Clouds *for* Dessert

SWEET TREATS
FROM THE WILD WEST

Thanks and Acknowledgments

For all their generous help in all kinds of ways, from
recipes to metalcraft, and from dishes to geology, I would like to thank
Edith Lowell, Lisa Cooper, Tracy Vega, Robin Stancliff, Jeannine Brookshire,
Tom Bredlow, Ardith Arnold, and Clark Arnold.

RIO NUEVO PUBLISHERS®
P.O. Box 5250, Tucson, Arizona 85703-0250
(520) 623-9558, www.rionuevo.com

Book Design: Karen Schober, Seattle, Washington

Library of Congress Cataloging-in-Publication Data

Lowell, Susan, 1950-
  Clouds for dessert : sweet treats from the Wild West / by Susan Lowell ; photography by Robin Stancliff.
     p. cm.
  ISBN 1-887896-58-9 (pbk.)
  1. Desserts--West (U.S.) 2. Cookery, American--Western style. 3. Cookery, American--Southwestern style. I.
Title.
  TX773.L69 2004
  641.8'6'0978--dc22
                                        2004002728

Printed in Korea

10 9 8 7 6 5 4 3 2 1

Clouds for Dessert

SWEET TREATS
FROM THE WILD WEST

SUSAN LOWELL

photography by
ROBIN STANCLIFF

RIO NUEVO PUBLISHERS
TUCSON, ARIZONA

Contents

Clouds for Dessert:
Sweet Treats from the Wild West

DID YOU EVER TASTE A CLOUD? Or take a bite out of the Grand Canyon? What if the West could taste the way it looks? Clearly, some of the great natural phenomena would have to be spectacular desserts.

And why not? Of all foods, surely desserts offer us the most fantasy and fun. The world is full of stories, and as a writer who also loves to cook I know some ways to tell them in flour, sugar, eggs, and fruit as well as in words and pictures. Some years ago, when my children were small, I translated the old English story of the Three Little Pigs into the modern Southwest where we live. In this cookbook I have translated that story (*The Three Little Javelinas*) once again—this time from words and pictures into gingerbread. And that's only the beginning. As you will see, a little kitchen magic can turn the Rocky Mountains into snowcapped sundaes, or prickly pear cactus fruit into ice pops, pancakes, and tender rosy pies. But how can you serve clouds for dessert?

First comes a story. When I was a child, I used to look up at the clouds in the Western sky and greedily dream that they were enormous puffs and swirls of whipped cream. But after many years of cooking, I see them now as meringues floating in the most exquisite of fruit sauces. The Grand Canyon, on the other hand, must be sliced from a layer cake, but not just any layer cake—a breathtakingly delicious and surprising one.

"*¿Hay postre?*" Those were my first words of Spanish, and some of my earliest in any language. "Is there any dessert?" my father used to ask my mother in Spanish at the end of a meal. He meant to talk over our little heads, but my brother and I understood perfectly, and we snapped those heads in our mother's direction. Dessert! We didn't always have it. Sometimes we lived in such remote places that we depended on dry and preserved foods for weeks at a time. Dessert, if it did magically appear, was often canned peaches, plums, or pears, a simple treat dating back to the times of wagons and prospectors, and my brother and I always happily scraped the last drops of vaguely fruity syrup from our dishes. But sometimes there were fancier desserts also based on pantry staples, such as Denver pudding and one-egg cake. Or the canned fruit might possibly be glorified into a crusty golden cobbler.

Two earth-shaking events occurred close together in my early life: first I learned to read, and then I received for Christmas a set of tiny baking pans and miniature cake, pie, and cookie mixes. I immediately produced a series of very sticky desserts three inches in diameter, which tasted like nothing else in the universe except maybe envelope glue. At the time I thought they were delectable, but in self-defense my mother quickly encouraged me to do real baking. The living room of the rented house where we lived in Prescott, Arizona, was lined with bookcases, and the bottom shelves were filled with children's books. So in the intervals between baking my first cakes, I used to lie on the floor and read, and read, and read. Food and language still fascinate me.

"Bitter! Bitter!" goes a famous Russian wedding toast, to which the response is: "Make it sweet!" And then the bride and groom must kiss. Associated with celebration, sweets are symbolic of joy and frivolity, of happy endings: comedy as opposed to tragedy. Can something as modest as a blob of custard lift us up and inspire us? The experience of collecting these recipes and writing this book shows me that it can. Can you bake a biography—tell the story of a life in sugar? Surely you could illustrate one: pink and blue baby cookies, a changing parade of birthday cakes, a graduation dessert baked in the shape of a mortarboard cap, wedding cake, chocolate pudding for a hospital patient, a golden anniversary cake, and the comfort of food after a funeral.

As I cook, story after story rises from the scribbled cards, the spotted cookbook pages, the pots and pans, and, above all, the colors, the aromas, and the tastes. Some I have recorded here; some I hope to tell in other books. Some you will only discover if you follow the recipes, for cooking is a tremendously powerful form of communication.

The best food of a region creates a sense of place as almost nothing else can. In his great novel *The Leopard*, Giuseppe di Lampedusa evokes a whole sensuous, melancholy Sicilian world as his main character contemplates a table of desserts served at a ball in Palermo around the year 1900:

> Huge blond *babas,* Mont Blancs snowy with whipped cream, cakes speckled with white almonds and green pistachio nuts, hillocks of chocolate-covered pastry, brown and rich as the Catanian plain,… pink ices, champagne ices, coffee ices, all parfaits … melody in major of crystallized cherries, acid notes of yellow pineapple, and those cakes called "triumphs of gluttony" filled with green pistachio paste…. (Translated by Archibald Colquhoun.)

History and memory merge in the flavors of food. This is also true of my own stomping ground, the lower left-hand quadrant of the United States. You could call it the American Southwest, or maybe "Baja West" might be better, since the state and international boundaries are somewhat difficult to define.

These are Western recipes (including numerous variations), some big on sugar and some not-so-sweet. They express our climates and geography (pomegranates and citrus from the desert, piñon-pine nuts and apples from the mountains) as well as our history and culture (the saguaro-cactus syrup of the Tohono O'odham Nation of southern Arizona and northern Mexico, Spanish *flan,* Texas cowboy cake, New Mexican *biscochitos,* and a very lush and chi chi chocolate mousse pie from the recent Southwest foodie period). Mostly, however, these homespun recipes represent a culture that knows how to make do. They call for common ingredients and require no high-level pastry-chef skills. There is no triumph of—or in—gluttony. Instead they produce what my daughter Mary calls "cookies made by real people."

And of course dessert does come *after;* we cannot live by sweets alone. Even in the Wild West, treats follow the serious business of nutrition. After the beef and the vegetables and the hot sun go down, then it's time for something a little special. For example, after traditional Christmas Eve tamales, what could be more festive than a nearly weightless spoonful of that fluffy pink, green, and white pudding called *almendrado?* Frozen lime chiffon pie dissolves deliciously on the tongue after a fiery meal of red chile stew. Creamy *natillas* cap the celebration of a New Mexico wedding. At the end of a children's party, the battered piñata swings over the circle of upturned faces, crashes into the stick one last time, and finally rains down its goodies far and wide. ¡Olé!

Ingredients, Measurements, and Techniques

FLOUR Unless otherwise specified, use all-purpose flour, either bleached or unbleached, for the recipes in this book. To measure, spoon flour lightly into a measuring cup, and level it with a straight edge. Each cup weighs 4.5 ounces. (Weighing is always the most accurate, but not always the most convenient, way to measure.)

SUGAR "Sugar" means white granulated sugar, unless a recipe indicates another kind. Measure it, as well as superfine or baker's sugar, by spooning out level cupfuls, each weighing 7 ounces. Spoon powdered sugar lightly into a measuring cup, and level it as well. Each cup of powdered sugar weighs 4 ounces. To measure brown sugar, pack it firmly into the cup; each level cup weighs 8 ounces.

EGGS These recipes are based on large eggs, which contain slightly more than 3 tablespoons of semi-liquid yolk and white. If egg safety is a problem in your area or if you cook for someone with health concerns, substitute pasteurized egg products in all recipes containing raw or lightly cooked eggs. Since pasteurized raw egg whites often do not whip satisfactorily, it's best to replace them in meringues and frostings with dried egg whites or with meringue powder (a dry egg-white and sugar mixture sold in cake-decorating departments). Reconstitute the egg white products according to the directions on the package.

CREAM In these recipes either regular whipping cream (30–36 percent butterfat) or heavy cream (over 36 percent butterfat) will work equally well.

BUTTER AND OTHER SHORTENINGS Unsalted butter allows precise salt measurement in cooking, but salted butter also works well. Generally, margarine can replace up to half of the butter in a recipe without serious loss of quality, but butter almost always tastes and functions better. However, vegetable shortening makes very tasty, very manageable pie crust and gingerbread cookie dough.

Specialty Ingredients

UNSWEETENED PRICKLY PEAR NECTAR Natalie McGee manufactures prickly pear juices and condiments for specialty markets, including health-conscious consumers. Prickly pear products may aid in the treatment of diabetes.

Arizona Cactus Ranch
P.O. Box 8
Green Valley, AZ 85622
520-625-4419
800-582-9903
www.arizonacactusranch.com

PRICKLY PEAR SYRUP Cheri's Desert Harvest produces delicious ruby-rose-colored cactus syrup. Along with the company's other products, it is widely distributed, but Cheri's also offers mail-order service.

Cheri's Desert Harvest
1840 East Winsett
Tucson, AZ 85713
800-743-1141
Fax: 520-623-7741
www.cherisdesertharvest.com

GHIRARDELLI SWEET GROUND CHOCOLATE AND COCOA This extra-rich chocolate powder is sold in supermarkets and specialty food shops, and by mail order. To find a supplier near you, contact:

Ghirardelli Chocolate Company
1111 139th Avenue
San Leandro, CA 94578-2631
800-877-9338
www.ghirardelli.com.

ANCHO CHILE POWDER Many excellent companies offer specialty chile products. Here are a few good sources for ancho powder, with descriptions of its flavor that reveal the wide variations that exist among peppers—and among tasters.

Chile Today–Hot Tamale
("The ancho will add a sweet plum/raisin-like flavor to dishes.")
31 Richboynton Road
Dover, NJ 07801
800-HOT-PEPPER
Fax: 973-537-2917

Da Gift Basket Chile Products of New Mexico (Ancho: "Deep red color and aromatic fruity taste.")
P.O. Box 2085
Los Lunas, NM 87031
505-865-3645
www.dagiftbasket.com

Native Seeds/SEARCH (Ancho: "A mild, sweet earthy taste … very versatile.")
526 North 4th Avenue
Tucson, AZ 85705
520-622-5561
www.nativeseeds.org

Pendery's World of Chiles & Spices
[Does not attempt to describe the flavor.]
1221 Manufacturing Street
Dallas, TX 75207
800-533-1870
www.penderys.com

Santa Cruz Chili & Spice Co. (Ancho: "Mild fruit flavor with tones of coffee, licorice, tobacco, dried plum, and raisin, with a little woodiness.")
P.O. Box 177
Tumacacori, AZ 85640
520-398-2591
www.santacruzchili.com

Sweet Freedom Farm ("We just started stocking a dark Ancho powder which is to die for. It's had all the seeds, stems, and membrane removed before powdering, and it's a nice, deep, dark rich color, and really aromatic and full of flavor … sort of a gourmet Ancho powder. Woo hoo!")
6724 Coors Boulevard S.W.
Albuquerque, NM 87121
505-873-9173
www.sweetfreedomfarm.com

Preparing Pans

Grease the bottoms and sides of cake pans with butter or shortening (not margarine), line them with wax paper cut to fit, and grease the paper. Next, dust the interior with 1–2 tablespoons of flour and knock out the excess flour. Or coat the inside surfaces with a flour-based baking spray, such as Baker's Joy, line with wax paper, and spray the paper.

Grease baking sheets—in most cases, even the supposedly nonstick type—lightly with butter, shortening, or flour spray. However, the new silicone pan liners create less work for a cook, and parchment paper or baking parchment is the easiest nonstick alternative of all. A single inexpensive sheet of this special cooking paper can be used to bake several pans of cookies, while the pan remains clean.

Mixing

Either a hand-held or a stationary electric mixer is a great help with jobs like creaming butter or beating egg yolks with sugar. It's nearly indispensable for whipping egg whites, particularly large quantities of them in meringues. The best substitute is a large balloon whisk, combined with a strong arm and a patient attitude.

Cookies

IT MAY BE POSSIBLE to live without cookies. A cookieless universe wouldn't collapse into a pile of space dust … but then again, maybe it would. What could ever fill their place? Cookies are one of the true elements of existence, a simple pleasure, modest and portable, inexpensive and versatile. Plain cookies demand little of the cook, except an oven. Even the humblest half-dozen looks festive when presented on a plate, and almost any kind makes a nice gift.

The first Western cookies were probably seventeenth-century Spanish *biscochitos* of the sort that are still baked and enjoyed, especially in New Mexico. Along with wave after wave of American settlement in the nineteenth century came the recipes and ingredients for many others, especially gingerbread and sugar cookies. According to her diary (dated from Flagstaff, Arizona, in July of 1903) my great-grandmother Emma Sykes made cookies and custard to celebrate my grandfather's seventh birthday. A slender figure in a white dress with leg-o'-mutton sleeves, she waits at the edge of my consciousness for her story to be told. Besides her diaries, we still possess *The Book of Household Management* by Isabella Beeton, which Emma brought with her from London to Arizona. She must have learned to make cookies in Flagstaff, as the staunch British Mrs. Beeton does not even mention them under "Breads, Biscuits, and Cakes."

By then the little sweet cakes or biscuits of many other regions—Europe, Latin America, Asia—were arriving in the West. The population explosion of the twentieth century also created a cookie explosion; most American favorites, including chocolate chip cookies and brownies, were invented within the last hundred years, and cookie creation still goes on and on. It's a craft that mingles a touch of sculpture, a dab of painting, a little bit of self-indulgence, and a few calories of sustenance. And maybe the lightest of messages. Read on: here's a little Western history and Western culture in a few sweet bites.

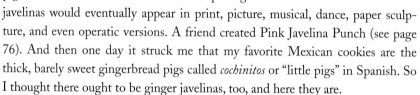

Ginger Cookies

When I first imagined a children's story about three little javelinas—and described them as "hairy Southwestern cousins of pigs"—I never dreamed that those enterprising javelinas would eventually appear in print, picture, musical, dance, paper sculpture, and even operatic versions. A friend created Pink Javelina Punch (see page 76). And then one day it struck me that my favorite Mexican cookies are the thick, barely sweet gingerbread pigs called *cochinitos* or "little pigs" in Spanish. So I thought there ought to be ginger javelinas, too, and here they are.

Gingerbread is easy. What's hard is finding a javelina cookie cutter! Eventually I drew my own design, and my friend Tom Bredlow kindly transferred it to metal for me. You can also substitute a pig cutter and remodel each pig's head and tail slightly by pinching the dough with your fingers. Tailless and skinny, with elongated heads, New World javelinas are technically called peccaries and are only distantly related to Old World swine, but the general outline is similar.

Once upon a time, gingerbread and cookies were almost synonymous. My grandmother Lavina Cumming Lowell's copy of the *Boston Cooking-School Cookbook* is dated 1922, and Chapter XXX is entitled "Gingerbreads, Cookies, and Wafers." Ginger dominates the first fourteen recipes, and many molasses-brown spots and fingerprints mark those well-used pages. Whether she cooked on Arizona ranches or in the jungles of Peru, my indomitable Grandmama made cake-like gingerbread more often than the rolled-cookie type, but as the cookbook author, Fannie Farmer, indicates, they are cousins under the crust.

One cold December in Denver when I was five years old, my mother took my brother and me to visit Mrs. Emma Bell, a famous baker of Christmas cookies. When she was a tiny child, probably before 1890, Mrs. Bell's family did their washing outdoors in a tub of boiling water over a fire, and one washday she badly burned and permanently crippled a hand. I remember her white hair and her kindness, but I don't remember her hand at all. Instead I remember watching enthralled, my nose at the height of the kitchen counter, as she deftly painted brilliant colors on ginger cookies, using a turkey feather as a brush.

Based on Mrs. Bell's thin, fine "Painted Cookies," as she called them, this easy recipe makes amusing Southwestern shapes such as chiles, coyotes, cacti, and special colorful cookie angels inspired by the marvelous paintings of Cynthia Miller.

MAKES ABOUT 4 DOZEN

1 cup molasses

½ cup vegetable shortening

1¼ teaspoons baking soda

1 egg, beaten

4 cups flour

2 teaspoons ginger

2 teaspoons ground cinnamon

½ teaspoon nutmeg

¼ teaspoon ground cloves

1 teaspoon salt

IN A LARGE SAUCEPAN over medium heat, warm the molasses and shortening until the shortening melts. Remove from the heat and add the soda and egg. In a medium bowl, whisk together the flour, ginger, cinnamon, nutmeg, cloves, and salt. Stir the dry ingredients into the first mixture, adding a little more flour if the dough seems too sticky. Turn it out onto a sheet of plastic wrap, form it into a ball, wrap it tightly, and refrigerate until chilled, 2–3 hours, or for as long as a week. (To store it more than a few hours, double-wrap the dough by sealing it inside a plastic bag.)

Preheat the oven to 350 degrees F. Dividing it into 3 or 4 batches, roll out the dough to a thickness of about ¼ inch on a lightly floured surface with a lightly floured rolling pin. Cut into various shapes. Bake on heavy, lightly greased cookie sheets for 7–10 minutes, switching the position of the cookie sheets from top to bottom midway through the baking time. Cool on wire racks, and frost and decorate the cookies as you like.

Mrs. Bell's Cookie Paint

3 cups powdered sugar

2 egg whites (please see note on eggs, page 9)

1 teaspoon lemon juice (and more if needed)

Food coloring, either liquid or paste

Sift the sugar into a medium mixing bowl. Lightly beat the egg whites in a small bowl, and add them to the sugar. Thin the icing to the consistency of paint with lemon juice, bearing in mind that liquid food coloring will thin it slightly more. Divide it into as many portions as you want colors, and tint each one. Remember to leave yourself some white paint! Paint the cooled ginger cookies with clean turkey feathers (or pastry brushes, clean new paint brushes, knives, or even very, very clean young fingers).

All-Purpose Decorating Icing

½ cup butter or margarine, softened

3½ cups powdered sugar

1 pinch salt

2 tablespoons milk or cream, plus more if needed

FLAVOR WITH:

1 teaspoon vanilla extract, or

½ teaspoon almond extract, or

1 tablespoon lemon juice and 1 teaspoon grated lemon zest, or

3 tablespoons orange juice and 1 teaspoon grated orange zest

Liquid or paste food coloring (optional)

Cream the butter or margarine in a large mixing bowl. Gradually add the powdered sugar, followed by the salt, enough liquid to reach the desired consistency, and the flavoring. For piping, the icing ought to be fairly stiff; for frosting and glazing, you need a more fluid consistency. Finally, add color to the icing, remembering that this may slightly thin the texture.

NOTE You can reduce the amount of butter substantially, and even omit it, especially if you want more of a glaze and less of a frosting. This molasses-flavored glaze closely matches the color of gingerbread itself, and it nicely sets off colored sugar or other additions.

VARIATION: BROWN GLAZE FOR GINGERBREAD Mix 1 tablespoon water with 1 cup powdered sugar, thin the frosting to the desired consistency, and color with droplets of molasses.

Frosting Tips

- A tablespoon or two of corn syrup will add gloss to an icing.
- Powdered sugar usually must be sieved or sifted to remove lumps.
- Paste food coloring provides more intense and varied hues than liquid color.
- A little lemon or orange extract enhances a citrus frosting.
- A few teaspoons of prickly pear syrup will give white icing a delicate flavor and a pretty lavender-pink color.

Piñon Shortbread

From pueblo to pueblo across the Southwest, Kokopelli the humpbacked flute player used to wend his way. According to Native American legend, he scattered gifts and happiness, as well as mischief and fertility, wherever he went. He played Don Juan among the women and sweet music to everyone, and when he blew into his flute (a nose flute, by the way), the sun shone, the snow melted, the plants sprouted, the birds sang, and the animals frisked.

And what did Kokopelli carry inside that hump? Accounts of the contents vary, but they include corn, beads, shells, blankets, moccasins, deerskin shirts … and babies. According to Navajo tradition, Kokopelli's hump bulged with clouds filled with rainbows and seeds. At San Ildefonso Pueblo he appeared as a wandering minstrel with a load of music on his back, who would trade new songs for old ones. Sometimes in these stories Kokopelli, a mega-Johnny Appleseed and perhaps a symbol for trade as well as spring, spreads the seeds of all the plants in all the world, and then, like the Music Man, leaves town.

Surely those seeds included tasty piñon nuts. Since time immemorial the inhabitants of the Southwest, from mouse to man, have raided piñon pinecones for their tiny brown nuts. They are good raw, but toasting brings out their subtle flavor. A modern Kokopelli might go far handing out these cookies.

MAKES ABOUT 2½ DOZEN COOKIES

½ cup piñon nuts or other pine nuts

2 cups flour

½ cup sugar

¼ teaspoon salt

1½ teaspoons ground cinnamon

1 cup butter, each stick cut into 8 pieces and slightly softened

TOAST THE PIÑON NUTS lightly in a small, heavy skillet over medium heat, or on a baking sheet in a 350-degree oven for 5–8 minutes, stirring several times.

When the nuts are cool, place them in a food processor with the flour, sugar, salt, and cinnamon. Pulse these ingredients together about 10 times, until the nuts are chopped and the mixture is uniform. Add the butter, processing just until the dough becomes a ball.

Dust a work surface and a rolling pin lightly with flour, and roll the dough out to a thickness of about ⅓ inch. Using a simple cutter, cut the dough into 2-inch cookies, and place them on baking sheets lined with parchment paper, or lightly greased. To maintain their neat shape, you must refrigerate or freeze the raw cookies for about an hour before baking (or wrap airtight and keep frozen for future use).

Preheat the oven to 300 degrees F. Bake the cookies for about 45 minutes (they are thick and the temperature is low), until they are firm but not browned. Allow them to cool for a few minutes on the baking sheets before moving them to a wire rack to cool completely. Wrapped airtight, they will keep for weeks, unless Kokopelli finds them.

If you don't have a food processor, pulverize the cooled pine nuts in a blender with the flour, sugar, salt, and cinnamon. Soften the butter, and cream it in a large mixing bowl until it is fluffy. Turn the mixer to low speed and gradually add the flour mixture. Roll, chill or freeze, and bake the dough as described above.

Gold Bars

MAKES ABOUT 4
DOZEN COOKIES

1½ cups flour

¼ teaspoon salt

1½ teaspoons baking powder

⅓ cup softened butter

¼ cup vegetable oil

¾ cup sugar

½ teaspoon orange extract

½ teaspoon almond extract

1 teaspoon vanilla extract

1 tablespoon orange juice

1–2 teaspoons grated orange zest
(from 1 orange)

1 egg

3–4 tablespoons yellow or gold
decorating sugar, or yellow
or gold edible glitter

The Gold Rush brought my father's family to California soon after 1849. After doing a certain amount of digging, one ancestor carefully reviewed his situation, and then he made all the gold he had found into a little necklace for his daughter and started a business supplying the miners, where he prospered. My cousin Diane Cooley has inherited the necklace, a small, simple gold cross on a chain.

I'd never say no to a Gold Rush necklace, but kitchen alchemy can turn plain old flour and sugar into treasure, too. This quick and easy recipe produces 48 delicious, glittering cookies in less than an hour.

PREHEAT THE OVEN to 375 degrees F. In a medium bowl, whisk together the flour, salt, and baking powder. Place the butter, oil, sugar, orange extract, almond extract, vanilla, orange juice, orange zest, and egg in a large mixing bowl. Beat these ingredients together until the mixture is fluffy and light. Add the flour mixture and beat well.

Spread the dough evenly in a lightly greased 15 x 10 x 1-inch baking pan, and sprinkle it generously with colored sugar or glitter. Bake until it turns golden brown, about 10–12 minutes. Let it cool for 5 minutes, and then cut it into 48 bars.

Biscochitos

Mildly flavored with anise and cinnamon, biscochitos (bee-sko-CHEE-tos) are a favorite holiday treat in New Mexico. A fleur-de-lis shape is traditional, but biscochitos—also spelled "bizcochitos"—appear in many forms, especially around Christmas time and other festive occasions. This recipe is based on one in Regina Romero's enchanting memoir, *Flora's Kitchen: Recipes from a New Mexico Family.*

In 1901, when she was fifteen years old, Flora Durán went for a walk around the plaza of Albuquerque's Old Town. Arm-in-arm with her two older sisters, Flora noticed an older man in a wide-brimmed hat, who was staring at her. Without saying a word, he handed her a bouquet of flowers and a box of candy and disappeared. "She told us many times that when she was a child she dreamed of becoming a Catholic nun," recalled her granddaughter Regina Romero. But soon the unknown suitor in the wide sombrero spoke to Flora's father.

"I had no choice," she told her granddaughters many years later, "even though I tried to tell my father that I wanted to go into the convent instead."

Her future husband, Melitón Romero, sent for his parents from Arizona "so that they could ask for me in the old way, *a pedir la mano* (to ask for my hand)," said Flora. "The ceremony is called *el prendorio*." After their parents completed the formal agreement, Flora and Melitón exchanged gifts, and the prendorio concluded with toasts over wine and biscochitos baked by Flora's grandmother, who was known in the family as *La Grande*.

"It was all very beautiful," Flora said. "But when your grandfather and his family left I went to the chapel at San Felipe Church and prayed to the Blessed Mother. I told her that I could accept that I would not become a nun.... I prayed that I could accept anything from this man, but that he not be a drinking man."

And so they married and became the parents of eleven children.

"You know?" said Flora to her granddaughters. "The Blessed Mother answered my prayer. Ohhh, yes! You see, your grandfather was everything else but ... a drinking man!"

MAKES ABOUT 3
DOZEN 3-INCH COOKIES

I tablespoon anise seed (or up to
2 tablespoons for a stronger
anise flavor)

3 tablespoons water

3½–3¾ cups flour

2½ teaspoons baking powder

½ teaspoon salt

I cup softened butter (for truly
authentic biscochitos, you ought
to use excellent fresh lard;
shortening is acceptable)

½ cup sugar

½ cup packed brown sugar

2 eggs

½ teaspoon anise extract
(optional)

FOR THE TOPS:

I teaspoon ground
cinnamon

⅓ cup sugar

IN A SMALL SAUCEPAN, simmer the anise seed in the water for 5 minutes, and allow this infusion to cool.

Meanwhile, in a medium bowl, whisk the flour with the baking powder and salt. In a large bowl, cream the butter with both kinds of sugar. When the mixture is fluffy, add the eggs, anise extract, and anise seed mixture. Gradually add the dry ingredients. Gather the dough into a ball, wrap it airtight, and chill it for at least an hour.

Preheat the oven to 350 degrees F. Mix the cinnamon with the remaining sugar in a small bowl.

Dust a work surface and rolling pin lightly with flour, and roll out the dough approximately ¼-inch thick and cut out 3-inch cookies. Dust the tops with cinnamon mixed with ⅓ cup sugar. (You may substitute colored decorating sugar, but you will lose the important flavor of cinnamon, which blends beautifully with anise.) Bake the biscochitos about 10 minutes, or until they are lightly browned around the edges, and then cool them on wire racks. They have very good keeping qualities.

Mexican Wedding Cakes

Does that little nut ball dribbling sugar down your shirt really have anything to do with Mexico or weddings? Nearly the same confection appears under many different names: Swedish teacakes, Russian teacakes, Portuguese wedding cakes, wedding bells, butterballs, nut butter balls, and *polvorones* or "dusties" in Spanish-speaking America. The story of Flora Durán's betrothal (see the Biscochitos recipe) does place small cakes among Hispanic wedding traditions in the Southwest, although she refers to a different cookie altogether.

The wedding-cake type of cookie may be made with almonds or walnuts instead of pecans, which are New World natives and still little-known in Europe. Pecans grow across the American South and West, where they tend to be the freshest, most readily available, and most popular nut in the market. To deepen the flavor here, I have added a little almond butter, which is available in specialty or health-food markets. If you want to keep your shirt clean, resist the temptation to make Mexican wedding cakes larger than bite-size.

**MAKES ABOUT 4½
DOZEN 1½-INCH COOKIES**

½ cup pecan halves

1 cup powdered sugar

¼ teaspoon salt

1 cup butter, each stick cut into 8
pieces and slightly softened

½ teaspoon vanilla extract

1¾ cups flour

1–2 cups powdered
sugar (for coating)

PLACE THE PECANS in a food processor with the 1 cup powdered sugar and salt, and process until the nuts are finely ground. Add the butter slices and process until the dough is smooth. Scrape down the sides of the bowl, add the vanilla, process briefly, and then add the flour, processing just until the dough forms a ball. Scrape the dough onto a large piece of plastic wrap. Seal the wrapped dough inside a plastic bag, and chill it for at least an hour.

Preheat the oven to 300 degrees F, and set the racks at the high and low positions.

Then form the dough into 1-inch balls, rolling them between your palms and occasionally dusting your hands with flour if necessary. Place the balls 1½ inches apart on ungreased or parchment-lined baking sheets. Bake them until they just begin to brown, about 15–20 minutes, reversing the baking sheets after 7 or 8 minutes.

These cookies are delicate. Allow them to cool on the pans for several minutes; then carefully roll them in powdered sugar while they are still warm. To look their best they may need two coats of sugar, and possibly another just before serving. Stored airtight, they last for about a month.

If you don't have a food processor, grind the pecans with the 1 cup powdered sugar in a blender until the nuts are very fine. Cream the softened butter with the nut-sugar mixture in a large mixing bowl until the texture is fluffy. Beat in the vanilla. Whisk the flour and salt together in a medium mixing bowl, and gradually add them to the butter mixture. Chill, shape, bake, and sugar the cookies as described above.

Mexican Chocolate Wedding Cakes

MAKES ABOUT 4½
DOZEN 1½-INCH COOKIES

I cup pecan halves

⅓ cup powdered sugar

½ cup Ghirardelli Sweet Ground
Chocolate, or cocoa powder

1¾ cups flour

¾ teaspoon ground cinnamon

¼ teaspoon salt

I cup butter, each stick cut into 8
pieces and slightly softened

I egg

2 teaspoons vanilla extract

½ cup powdered sugar

¼ cup Ghirardelli Sweet Ground
Chocolate, or cocoa powder

Mexico is the homeland of chocolate, which was known to the Aztecs as *choco-latl*. Chocolate aficionados still order it prepared to their specifications in the open markets of Oaxaca, where the rich brown goo oozes out of grinders, already blended with sugar, almonds, and cinnamon—a heavenly combination. What could be more appropriate than chocolate Mexican wedding cakes?

This recipe calls for Ghirardelli Sweet Ground Chocolate and Cocoa, a unique product of that grand old California chocolate company. One of the highlights of my freshman year at Stanford was my first visit to Ghirardelli Square in San Francisco, where a working chocolate factory still swishes and splashes the magical brown liquid right under your nose. But if you can't find Ghirardelli's, plain cocoa powder will do.

PLACE THE PECANS in a food processor with ⅓ cup powdered sugar, and process until the nuts are finely ground. In a medium mixing bowl, whisk together ½ cup chocolate or cocoa with the flour, cinnamon, and salt.

Next, add the butter slices to the pecans and sugar in the processor, and process until the dough is smooth. Scrape down the sides of the bowl, add the egg and the vanilla, process briefly, and then add the chocolate-and-flour mixture, processing just until the dough forms a ball. Scrape the dough onto a large piece of plastic wrap. Seal the wrapped dough inside a plastic bag, and chill it for at least an hour.

Preheat the oven to 325 degrees F. and set the racks at the high and low positions.

Then form the dough into 1-inch balls, rolling them between your palms and occasionally dusting your hands with flour if necessary. Place the balls 1½ inches apart on ungreased or parchment-lined baking sheets. Bake them until they are barely firm, about 15–18 minutes, reversing the baking sheets after 7 or 8 minutes. Meanwhile, in a small bowl blend the remaining powdered sugar with the remaining ¼ cup chocolate or cocoa.

These cookies are very delicate. Allow them to cool on the pans for several minutes; then carefully roll them in the chocolate powdered sugar while they are still warm. To look their best they may need 2 coats of sugar, and possibly another just before serving. Stored airtight, they last for about a month. They are excellent served with coffee or tea.

If you don't have a food processor, grind the pecans with the ⅓ cup powdered sugar in a blender until the nuts are very fine. Cream the softened butter with the nut-sugar mixture in a large mixing bowl until the texture is fluffy. Beat in the egg and the vanilla. Whisk the ½ cup chocolate or cocoa, flour, cinnamon, and salt together in a medium mixing bowl, and gradually add the dry ingredients to the butter mixture. Chill, shape, bake, and sugar the cookies as described above.

Sculpture Cookies

MAKES ABOUT 2 CUPS OF DOUGH

⅔ cup butter or margarine

⅓ cup sugar

½ teaspoon almond extract

1⅔ cups flour

Liquid food coloring

Cookie decorations, such as colored sugar, nuts, raisins, candy, etc. (optional)

Unlike a certain children's modeling clay, which has been scented deliberately to disgust young tasters, this colorful dough is deliciously edible and bakes into excellent cookies. But sculpting them is probably more fun than eating them, and even toddlers can participate.

PREHEAT THE OVEN to 300 degrees F. Cream the butter and sugar together in a large mixing bowl, and when the mixture is light and fluffy, add the almond extract. Gradually add the flour, and beat until you have a dry, crumbly mixture. Divide it into as many parts as you want colors, and add food coloring to each portion, kneading and squeezing with your hands until the dough is smooth and workable.

Form the cookies with your fingers, or by rolling and cutting. For structural strength, make them fairly thick (from ¼ to ¾ inches), and for the most striking cookies, use at least two different colors. To create interesting textures and shapes, experiment with kitchen tools such as forks, graters, and garlic presses. Add any other typical cookie decorations that you like.

Bake for 20–25 minutes on parchment or lightly greased baking sheets. The cookies should be firm to the touch but not at all brown, since that would detract from the other colors.

Gingerbread Adobe Dream Casa

MAKES 1 HOUSE
(ABOUT 6 X 6 X 9 INCHES), WITH
ENOUGH EXTRA GINGERBREAD
DOUGH TO MAKE SEVERAL
COOKIE FIGURES OR
REPLACEMENT PARTS

My spicy little house was inspired in part by Jim Harris's illustrations for *The Three Little Javelinas*, where the third javelina builds herself a small Southwestern showplace, complete with javelina family portraits and a copy of the Mona Lisa on the wall. And once you've made gingerbread javelinas, it's obvious that they should have a gingerbread house.

This house also draws on much older memories of a gingerbread cottage that glittered on the cover of a small square book, looking real yet oddly inedible. (Later I realized that the illustrations were photographs of a puppet show.) Nevertheless the house had tempted Hansel and Gretel to break off tasty bits of window shutter and doorknob. They didn't see the wicked witch who lurked behind the candy wall, but she saw them. It was a truly miraculous book, for it also played a song when it was set on our small turntable: "Nibble, nibble, little mousie!" croaked a scratchy voice. "Who's that eating up my housie?"

Deeply, madly, terribly I wanted to read that book, but I didn't know how. It was awful; I couldn't wait to learn. But that wouldn't happen until I entered first grade a few months later. So again and again I asked my slightly older friend Karen to read *Hansel and Gretel* aloud as we huddled together in my bottom bunk bed, poring over the pictures of grinning golden-haired puppets, real spilled milk, and strange twiggy German brooms. The ending never failed to satisfy us thoroughly: even a little puppet girl could bake a witch! And all the gingerbread kids who stood imprisoned in the witch's dreadful fence came back to life again.

Gingerbread is the perfect building medium for a Santa Fe-style house. It's exactly the right color and texture to suggest the traditional sun-dried mud bricks of the American Southwest. These are merely general guidelines because creativity reigns in the Land of Enchanted Gingerbread. Although it does take some time, a gingerbread house does not demand advanced cooking or craft skills, and all results are guaranteed to be spectacular—and good to eat. With a little help, even very young children can participate with great enjoyment and success in this delicious construction project. Four-year-olds quickly become adept with bags of frosting, and I know a twelve-year-old who built a scale model of the Great Pyramid of Khufu in gingerbread, entirely on her own.

Side walls (cut 2): 5½ x 9 inches

End walls (cut 2): 5½ x 5 inches

Roof (cut 1): 8¾ x 4¾ inches

Door (cut 1): 1½ x 2½ inches

Optional window (cut 1): 1½ x 1½ inches

Optional porch roof (cut 1): 8 x 2 inches

PLANNING AHEAD It's easiest to break up the process of building a gingerbread adobe house into several steps spread out over several days.

1. Imagine your house, and make or trace your pattern (a sample one is included here). Gather your ingredients, decor, and baking, decorating, and building equipment. This part takes at least several hours.

2. Mix the gingerbread adobe dough, and bake the house shapes. This process requires 1–2 hours.

3. Mix the mortar (also known as Royal Icing) and assemble the house, which will take from 30 minutes to an hour, depending on its complexity.

4. Finally, lay out the adornments you have chosen, mix more mortar, and start decorating. The time required for this stage may vary from 10 minutes for a preschooler to many sweet, sticky hours for a dedicated artist in sugar.

THE DESIGN A simple, rectangular adobe house consists of four walls and a flat roof. First, since accurate right angles are important, especially for corners, draw the pattern pieces on graph paper. Then transfer them to something more substantial, such as light cardboard or, better still, clear plastic, such as an inexpensive plastic placemat or shelf-lining material. Label all the pieces, and save them for reuse.

To make openings for rafters in the side walls, draw a line across the top of the pattern piece ½ inch down from the top edge and ½ inch in from the sides. Then evenly space five points along this line. Center a nickel coin below each point on the line, so that a ½-inch margin of dough will remain when the wall is cut, and trace around the nickel 5 times. Punch a hole in the pattern at the center of each nickel-sized circle. Later you will use the nickel again when you cut out the circles of dough.

Baking Equipment
- 2 baking sheets, either completely flat, rimless ones or jelly-roll pans
- Rolling pin
- Dishtowel
- Cutting board or other flat object slightly smaller than a jelly-roll pan (you will need this to brace an inverted jelly-roll pan while you roll out the dough on the back side; otherwise the pressure of the rolling pin will bend the pan and the gingerbread)
- Sharp cooking or craft knife
- Optional: small cookie cutters (for making doors and windows)

Assembly and Display Equipment
- Meringue powder (available from some supermarkets and all cake-decorating suppliers)
- Base for the house (either a tray, board, or sheet of Styrofoam 1 inch thick and at least 4 inches wider than the house all around, or approximately 1 foot square)
- "Feet" for the base, such as small cubes of Styrofoam (they make lifting and handling much easier)
- Optional lighting kit (available in craft stores and shops carrying equipment for dollhouses and Christmas model villages)

Decorating Equipment

Supermarkets often carry many of these modestly priced items. Craft, party, and cake-decorating stores nearly always stock them, and they are easily available from catalogues and over the Internet.

- Decorating bags (disposable plastic ones are easiest)
- Couplers and decorating tips for the bags (these gadgets may come with your disposable-bag kit, but it's useful to have at least two different tips, a large plain or "dot" tip and a large star tip, and decorating possibilities increase if you have two sizes of each)
- Candy (not chocolate, unless the house will be eaten very soon), such as hard candies, rock candy, gumdrops, lollipops, caramels, Necco wafers, peppermint candy canes, Red Hots, silver and gold dragées, Life Savers, and Tootsie Rolls
- Other edible decor, such as pretzels, cinnamon sticks, dry cereal, cookies, crackers, marshmallows, colored sugar, edible glitter, ice cream cones, and sugar cubes
- Large pretzel rods or breadsticks for *vigas,* or rafters
- Inedible decorations, such as miniature cars and toys

Good Strong Adobe Gingerbread

1 cup vegetable shortening
1 cup sugar
1 cup dark molasses
1 tablespoon ground ginger
1 teaspoon ground nutmeg
1 teaspoon ground cinnamon
1 teaspoon baking soda
$\frac{1}{2}$ teaspoon salt
$4\frac{1}{2}$–5 cups flour

Preheat the oven to 375 degrees F.

Melt the shortening, sugar, and molasses together in a large saucepan over low heat, stirring occasionally. Remove the pan from the heat and add the spices, baking soda, and salt. Mix thoroughly. Then blend in the flour, 1 cup at a time. When you have added 4 cups of flour, turn the dough out on a work surface and knead in the remaining flour until the dough is uniform in color and smooth and workable to the touch, neither sticky nor crumbly. Wrap two-thirds of it tightly in plastic to keep it moist while you work with the remaining third.

The dough rolls best when freshly made and still warm. But at this point you may also refrigerate it for up to 2 weeks, or freeze it for up to 3 months. Return it to room temperature, and knead it again until it is smooth before rolling it out. If it seems dry, either knead in several tablespoons of warm water by hand, or crumble the dough into a large mixer bowl, add water, and beat until the dough holds together and rolls well. To speed the process, you may warm dough for about 10 seconds in a microwave oven, but be very careful not to overheat it.

The next step is to roll out and cut the dough directly on the pan. First, either place a flat, rimless cookie sheet on a dampened dishtowel (to keep it from slipping), or reverse a rimmed jelly-roll pan over a cutting board or other flat brace, also placed on a damp towel.

Roll out a third of the gingerbread dough to an even thickness of about ¼ inch, working slowly and carefully to avoid the need to patch (but if you must patch, consider it a realistic rustic touch in the finished house). As the dough thins out, it becomes more malleable, and it will cover most of the pan. Be careful not to use too much flour.

Leaving at least ½ inch between pattern pieces, since the dough will spread as it bakes, lay your pattern on the dough, and cut around the pieces with a sharp knife or craft knife. To make the viga holes, first mark the centers of each one by pricking the dough through the pattern piece. Then remove the pattern and center a well-washed nickel over each mark, cutting around it with a small, sharp knife and removing the circles of dough as you go. If you want open doors and windows, cut them out now with pattern pieces or small cookie cutters. You can also simply mark the outlines and leave the dough to bake inside the cut. Lift out the excess dough, and wrap it for the next rolling. Bake the cookies for 10–15 minutes, testing for firmness to the touch (a fingertip should leave no print). The baked color will be a warm adobe brown, and the gingerbread will have spread slightly out of shape.

Remove the cookies from the oven, immediately lay the pattern pieces over them, hold them steady, protecting your hand with an oven mitt, and trim the cookies back into shape. You must do this very quickly, while the gingerbread is still soft. If necessary, re-warm the cookies briefly in the hot oven, but this is always tricky. As soon as they are cool enough to handle, very carefully remove them from the baking sheet to cool completely on a wire rack. For safe storage afterward, they should lie on a flat surface, wrapped airtight and well away from humidity, until construction time.

Proceed in the same way with the rest of your dough.

ASSEMBLY First prepare your base by gluing on its feet, and, using your pattern as a guide, mark a line where you wish the front of the house to be. Next, test the fit of your cookie pieces by holding them side by side. If you need to straighten any lines or remove any rough edges, very gently shave the gingerbread with the edge of a serrated knife, a metal nail file, or an emery board. Icing will correct and cover small irregularities.

Lay out the cookies with their better-looking sides up; you probably want to display these on the outside of the house. If you wish to light your house, now is the time to cut a hole in your base for the bulb and to plan the layout of the electrical cord. If the base is raised on feet, the cord fits nicely underneath; otherwise you must make a groove of some kind so the house will stand flat.

Meringue Powder Icing
(you will need approximately 2 batches per house)

4 cups (1 pound) powdered sugar

3 tablespoons meringue powder

$\frac{1}{3}$ to $\frac{1}{2}$ cup (6–8 tablespoons) warm water

Paste food coloring (optional)

In a large mixing bowl, combine at low speed the sugar, meringue powder, and about 6 tablespoons of the water. Then beat at high speed for 5–7 minutes, or until the icing holds stiff peaks that curve slightly at the tips. If you are a beginner, test a small amount in your decorating bag. If the mixture seems too stiff to push through a decorating tip, add more water by very small amounts, and test again. For intricate work, such as tiny stand-alone stars, you want a stiff icing, but for general purposes, you want one that squeezes fairly easily. While you are working with it, keep the icing tightly covered by pressing plastic wrap directly onto it. If you keep it overnight, you must store it in an airtight container, and you must re-beat it for a minute or two before using it. Add coloring when the basic texture is right.

NOTES ON COLOR White icing is the most versatile. It makes good snow and icicles, it sets off the colors of gingerbread and candy, and it can be used for assembly as well as decoration. However, if you want to assemble with adobe-colored icing that closely matches the gingerbread, tint each batch with 1–2 teaspoons of brown paste food coloring and $\frac{1}{8}$ teaspoon of copper paste food coloring, beating until uniform in color. For other colors, such as red and green, add paste food coloring until you achieve the tone you want. Liquid food coloring will make the icing too runny. Typical Santa Fe colors: blue and turquoise for doors and windows; pink; deep red; and earth tones, including ginger, cinnamon, molasses, chocolate, and vanilla.

In order to practice with your icing and to speed the later stages of construction, particularly if young cooks are involved, you might wish to make a few items in advance, such as Christmas trees, snowmen, other landscaping features, and furniture and decor for the inside of the house. Whenever you work with decorating equipment, be prepared to unclog the tips periodically with round wooden toothpicks, and also to wash them out from time to time. A few suggestions follow on making trees, fireplaces, and furniture, but of course your own imagination rules.

BUILDING It's really hard to make a mistake here. Even very small children can produce gorgeous houses, for icing covers up almost every slip, and candy distracts the eye from irregularities. Real houses aren't perfect either! And besides, fantasy and enjoyment are the goals with gingerbread dream casas.

You will need

- Gingerbread house pieces
- Icing (1 batch)
- Pretzel rods or breadsticks for wooden rafters, or vigas
- Pretzel rods, breadsticks, or peppermint sticks for porch supports

BASE Remember, this sounds more complicated than it is. Attach a large plain (or dot) tip to a decorating bag, position the empty bag in a container such as a tall drinking glass to hold it stable, and fill the bag half to two-thirds full with icing, tinted or not. Twist the bag tightly shut and either hold it that way or use a twist tie. Then, squeezing from the top, not the middle, and holding the bag at a 45-degree angle, pipe a thick, neat line of icing (about $3/8$-inch wide and equally deep) along the bottom edge of the front section of the gingerbread house, and set the cookie on the guideline that you have previously marked on your base. Stand it up straight and brace it between two small cans or jars of spice. The meringue mortar sets up very quickly, so these braces can be removed in a few minutes.

Meanwhile, run a line of icing along the bottom of a side section, and then another line along its front edge. Gently join the side piece to the front piece, making a neat right angle. No further bracing should be necessary.

Using the same technique, attach the second side, followed by the back piece. For optional reinforcement, run another line of icing around the inside bottom edge of the house shell, like the baseboard of a room, and also reinforce the four inside corner joints of the house.

If you have cut windows in your walls and plan to decorate and perhaps light the inside of your house, now is the time. Pop in your decorations, which you may want to make beforehand, and glue them all securely in place with the trusty decorating icing. Here are a few suggestions:

To make a Christmas tree, decorate an ice cream cone, either a sugar cone or a cup-style one, with patterns of green icing; tiny candies make good ornaments. Sometimes colored cup-style cones are available, including pale green. Around the base of the tree you may also wish to position presents made of candies in wrappers, or other appropriate items.

"Yum!" says chef Amelia Diane Hassen, aged 4½. (Photo by Mary Humphreys)

An adobe fireplace adds a whimsical touch. Start with a cup-style cone and carefully carve out a hemispherical fire opening with a small serrated knife. Ice the cone to a smooth surface with "snow" decorating icing (see recipe on page 34). Allow it to dry. For your fire, either make a pile of small pretzel sticks, broken to fit and "glued" in place, or a heap of rock candy crystals to simulate coals, with bits of colored tissue paper or cellophane for flames. If you are really ambitious, you can position your tiny lightbulb to illuminate the coals or flames in the fireplace. Or you can make it a shade and call it a lamp, or position it on top of your tree.

To make Navajo and Spanish weavings for the floor or the walls, pipe patterns of colored frosting on a few thin, flat cookies or crackers. Simple stripes and zigzags are the easiest.

For furniture you can construct a typical Southwestern *banco*, or built-in bench, by gluing small crackers together with icing and then smoothly coating the whole banco with more frosting. Or leave it rough and rustic.

Now install the pretzel vigas across the house, forming rafters. Arrange them so that they protrude from the walls about half an inch on each side of the house, and secure the vigas in place by piping icing around each joint, or leave them loose.

To roof the house, apply a generous stripe of icing around all the edges of the flat roof section and carefully lay it on top of the vigas. This will form a parapet around the upper edge. Like all flat roofs, this one may fail if it is forced to bear much weight or moisture, so probably the most ornamentation it can take is a peppermint-stick chimney above the fireplace, a row of caramel luminarias, and a dusting of sugar snow. Save the candy tiles for pitched roofs; you have many other decorative possibilities here.

Finally, install the optional front porch. The supports, either made of pretzel rods, breadsticks, or peppermint sticks, should be measured and cut before you start. To cut pretzels, breadsticks, or candy, score around the stick and break it at the scored place. First attach a supporting pillar upright against the wall at each end of the front of the house. Then run a generous line of icing along the back edge of the porch roof and gently press it into place on top of the supports. Brace it with cans or other items until the icing hardens; meanwhile you can set the front-porch pillars in place, beginning with one at each front corner, and using icing to secure each one at top and bottom.

At this point, the structure should be solid, so you can wait a day or two before you undertake the final decoration, if you wish.

DECORATING THE DREAM CASA Assemble your collection of candy and other decorative items. Mix a fresh batch of icing. (If necessary, you can make another batch later in the process.) Fill several decorating bags half to two-thirds full with different colors, if you are using them, and let your imagination run wild.

Just a thought or two: candy-cane pillars add a festive touch to the corners of the house and cover crooked seams of icing. Typically, doors and windows form focuses of decoration. There's always room for holiday decorations, such as wreaths, swags, garlands, and stars piped with icing and studded with candy. A few landscaping features, such as lollipop trees, add a great deal, as do fences, paths, doormats, mailboxes, and woodpiles. Remember, too, that you can cover any flaws and tie the whole little scene together with a final finishing coat of frosting, either left white to serve as snow, or sprinkled with brown raw sugar to imitate earth.

To enhance the Wild Western atmosphere, here are a few more suggestions:

- Hang a string, or *ristra*, of red chiles (made from icing) by the front door.
- Set up a row of caramels to serve as luminarias, also called *farolitos*, or brown-paper-bag lanterns.
- Make rustic wooden doors and "coyote fences" from rows of pretzel sticks.
- Plant candy cacti in the yard.
- Make flowerpots from stacks of Life Savers glued together with frosting.
- Build stone walls from nuts or candy rocks.
- Construct a tiny outdoor bread oven, or *horno*, from an ice cream cup cut to shape and stuccoed with icing.
- Build a little garden shrine from another ice cream cup.
- Make a rustic kiva ladder from pretzel rods glued together with frosting.
- Add a small toy pickup or horse-drawn wagon, or other appropriate figurines.

FINISHING TOUCHES When you think your design is nearly complete, but before you install any fences or tricky landscaping, it's time to mix up more frosting, if necessary, and create a snowstorm.

Snow Icing

Any leftover white icing, or a fresh batch

Water

White corn syrup

One teaspoon at a time, mix equal parts water and corn syrup into the icing. The amount will vary according to the dryness of the icing. Add just enough liquid to make an easy spreading consistency and one that will hold realistic icicle shapes.

Now spread frosting "snow" around the house, beginning close to the foundation and moving outward, section by section, as you cover the base and fill in any gaps in the decoration. Now is the time to build fences and lay patios. Make little drifts and swirls in the snow, and, if you wish, dribble the mixture from the roof and trees to create icicles.

This scene is not unrealistic: even the Sonoran Desert, home of the giant saguaro cactus, occasionally sees snow and ice. But if you want a warm, brown winter wonderland, omit the icicles and sprinkle the smooth wet frosting thickly with raw sugar. Regular brown sugar is too moist for this purpose, but raw sugar crystals make delicious Western dust. A bit of cotton, teased into wisps and anchored in place with a dab of icing, gives the illusion of smoke coming from the candy chimney. And for an even more dreamlike appearance, sprinkle the whole scene with plenty of edible glitter.

Cakes

"SOME PEOPLE DON'T REALIZE the importance of cake," said my young friend Kelsey, who at seventeen is already a serious cook. "Cake," she added firmly, "is *needed*."

She's right, I think. If you want a single memorable confection, a lighthearted and temporary monument to an occasion, there is nothing like a cake. Edible beauty—a trophy you never have to dust—what could be better? And somehow cookies or puddings, delightful as they both can be, just don't have the power of cakes to culminate the celebration of a birthday or a wedding.

Of course not all cakes are fancy. Quite often they are best unfrosted, especially when you want something delicious to tuck into a backpack and then consume while you sit on a rock at the top of a mountain. (And is it "frosting" or "icing"? As far as I can discover, these terms are interchangeable.) For actual eating while you hike the Grand Canyon, I recommend a nice sturdy pumpkin cake. To celebrate your triumphant return from rafting the Colorado River, a multilayer Grand Canyon ice cream extravaganza (page 113) might be *needed*.

Texas Cake

This Western delight turns up with a variety of names, including "Cowboy Cake," but "Texas Cake" suits it to a T. It's gigantic, flat, resilient, rich but folksy, and a bit over the top. (It's also easy!) So it makes a great gooey contribution to a bake sale or a potluck like the ones our ranch-conservation group regularly holds in Arizona's Altar Valley. Half a recipe produces eight generous servings—and it just fills a cake pan in the shape of Texas that I bought years ago when we lived in Dallas. The pan was a lot more portable than some of the other patriotic Texana—including swimming pools and stepping stones—that tickled my fancy, even though I'm an Arizonan.

Next time you need a big popular dessert, try this Texas of a cake. It's mighty fine, as they say there.

MAKES 16–20 SERVINGS

2 cups flour

2 cups sugar

¾ teaspoon salt

1 cup butter

¼ cup cocoa

1 cup water

½ cup buttermilk (or ½ cup regular milk mixed with 1 teaspoon vinegar)

2 eggs

1 teaspoon baking soda

1 teaspoon vanilla extract

GREASE AND FLOUR A PAN approximately 16 x 10 x 2 inches. Some recipes call for a 1-inch-deep jelly-roll pan or cookie sheet, but a deeper roasting pan is safer and easier to transport. A smaller, deeper pan such as one 13 x 9 x 2 inches will also work, but the baking time will approximately double.

Preheat the oven to 350 degrees F.

Whisk the flour, sugar, and salt together in a large mixing bowl. Put the butter, cocoa, and water in a medium-sized saucepan and bring them to a boil. Pour the hot mixture over the dry ingredients and beat the batter smooth with a mixer or a whisk. (Set the saucepan aside to make the icing.) Then add the buttermilk or sour milk, eggs, baking soda, and vanilla, and mix well. Pour the batter into the prepared pan and bake for 20–30 minutes, or until lightly springy in the center; a cake tester inserted in the center should come out clean. Set the cake in its pan on a rack and cool it briefly before adding the icing, which should be started about 5 minutes before the cake comes out of the oven.

Icing

½ cup butter

¼ cup cocoa

¼ teaspoon salt

6 tablespoons milk

1 pound powdered sugar (1 box or 4 cups)

2 teaspoons vanilla extract

Using the same saucepan as before, bring the butter, cocoa, salt, and milk to a boil, stir them well, and remove the pan from the heat. Add the powdered sugar and vanilla and beat until the sugar is dissolved. Pour this thin icing over the warm cake and allow it to cool and set before serving. Texas Cake keeps very well for several days.

One-Egg Cake

This was the first cake I learned to bake, probably about the time in second grade that I discovered to my joy that some books came in series. Seven Little House books! Ten Betsy-Tacy books! Vast numbers of Nancy Drew books! I devoured them all. In the Betsy-Tacy series, Tacy's mother often bakes a plain sheet cake that she sends with the two little girls on picnics. I always used to think that Tacy's mother's cake must be like this one-egg cake, which whips together in a flash from a few standard ingredients. Within an hour a small, golden, home-made cake or a dozen puffy cupcakes will appear in your kitchen. One-egg cake is good plain, sprinkled with powdered sugar, or topped with almost any flavor of frosting. It makes fine strawberry shortcake, and it dresses up beautifully in the Grand Canyon Ice Cream Cake (see page 113).

MAKES 6–12 SERVINGS

1½ cups (6 ounces) cake flour, sifted before measuring (or 1⅓ cups all-purpose flour)

¼ teaspoon salt

2 teaspoons baking powder

⅔ cup sugar

½ cup milk

¼ cup vegetable oil (or ¼ cup butter)

I egg

½ teaspoon vanilla extract

PREHEAT THE OVEN to 350 degrees F. For a sheet cake, grease and flour either an 8 x 8-inch or a 7 x 11-inch pan. For a round cake, grease, flour, and line with paper a 9-inch round cake pan. For cupcakes, grease and flour or line with paper liners a dozen cupcake tins.

Whisk the flour, salt, baking powder, and sugar together in a medium mixing bowl. In a small mixing bowl, beat together the milk, oil, egg, and vanilla. Or, in a small saucepan, melt the butter in the milk, allow the mixture to cool, and beat in the egg and vanilla. Blend the milk mixture into the dry ingredients, and beat well. Bake until the cake is lightly springy and a tester comes out clean (about 20 minutes for cupcakes and 25–30 minutes for larger cakes).

Madeleines

"A shudder ran through me," recalls the narrator of Marcel Proust's novel *Remembrance of Things Past.* "An exquisite pleasure had invaded my senses."

He has just tasted a "squat, plump little cake" called a madeleine, dipped in tea. "I feel something start within me," continues Proust's narrator rather alarmingly, "something that leaves its resting-place and attempts to rise...." Fortunately, what rises is only nostalgia, triggering a million and a half words of French prose.

These little cakes, however, are my grandfather's madeleines and probably spring from memories of his British youth. They are not Proust's pastries but stout, buttery cakes that evoke Victorian tea parties. They require no special culinary equipment, just a muffin pan. A man of great delicacy and kindness, my grandfather was a lifelong Western campfire cook who could bake a cake in a Dutch oven. His madeleines hint at a world far away from Proust's Parisian one. After war broke out in 1914, my grandfather "took the King's shilling" one day on London Bridge and enlisted in the British Army. Because he volunteered to serve in Ireland rather than Flanders, his recipe is here today.

"But when from a long-distant past nothing subsists," continues Proust, "after the people are dead, after the things are broken and scattered, taste and smell alone, more fragile but more enduring, more insubstantial, more persistent, more faithful, remain posted a long time, like souls, remembering, waiting, hoping, amid the ruins of all the rest, and bear unflinchingly, in the tiny and almost impalpable drop of their essence, the vast structure of recollection." (Translated by C. K. Scott Moncrieff and Terence Kilmartin.)

MAKES 12

3 eggs
½ cup sugar
1 cup flour
¼ teaspoon salt
½ teaspoon baking powder
1 teaspoon vanilla extract
½ cup butter, melted and cooled
About 2 tablespoons sugar

PREHEAT THE OVEN to 425 degrees F. Grease and flour 12 muffin cups, or line them with paper liners.

Beat the eggs and ½ cup sugar together in a large mixing bowl until the mixture is very light and fluffy. In a small bowl, whisk together the flour, salt, and baking powder, and then fold the dry ingredients into the egg mixture. Blend in the vanilla and melted butter. Fill cups half full with batter, and sprinkle the tops evenly with the 2 tablespoons sugar.

Bake 10–12 minutes, or until golden brown and lightly springy to the touch. Cool the madeleines on a wire rack, and decorate them, if you wish, with the optional frosting and cherries. I prefer them plain.

Icing (optional)

1 cup powdered sugar

1 tablespoon fresh lemon juice

12 candied cherries for decoration

In a small mixing bowl, blend the sugar with the lemon juice. Add more juice if necessary to make a thin frosting. After icing them, top each madeleine with a cherry.

Pumpkin Cake

This golden-brown autumnal treat is slightly adapted from a recipe in Kim Nelson's lovely book, *Southwest Kitchen Garden*, which also includes useful tips on growing your own pumpkins. Since pumpkin vines sprawl far and wide, Kim suggests planting them along the edges of your lawn or garden, or in tree wells. "Pumpkins are exciting and rewarding if children help in the garden," she points out. And children will also enjoy turning last night's jack-o-lantern into pumpkin cake. Unfrosted and nutritious, it's an excellent choice to pack in lunches or take on picnics. For a less sweet version, omit the raisins or chocolate chips.

MAKES 2 LARGE LOAVES OR 1 LARGE BUNDT CAKE

3⅓ cups all-purpose flour

3 cups sugar

½ teaspoon baking powder

2 teaspoons baking soda

1½ teaspoons salt

1 teaspoon ground cinnamon

½ teaspoon ground cloves

1 cup chopped walnuts or pecans

1⅓ cups raisins (or chocolate chips), optional

2 cups pumpkin puree (your own or canned)

⅔ cup softened butter

2 eggs

⅔ cup water

LINE WITH WAX PAPER, grease, and flour 2 large (6-cup) loaf pans, or grease and flour 1 large (12-cup) Bundt pan. Preheat the oven to 325 degrees F.

In a large mixing bowl, whisk together the flour, sugar, baking powder, baking soda, salt, cinnamon, and cloves. Add the nuts, raisins or chocolate chips, pumpkin, butter, eggs, and water. Beat together well, but do not overmix.

Pour the batter into the prepared pan or pans and bake for 1–1½ hours, or until the texture is slightly springy and a cake tester inserted in the center comes out clean. Let the cake cool for at least 15 minutes before removing it from the pan to a wire rack. Cut it when it is completely cool.

Serve it plain or with whipped cream. Pumpkin cake, wrapped, may be stored at room temperature for a week or in the freezer for up to 6 months.

Pumpkin Cake, Popcorn Nuggets (see page 63), and
Chocolate Popcorn (see page 63)

Dallas Dobosh Torte

SERVES 8

1 medium, high-quality pound cake, thawed if frozen

1 small package (6 ounces) chocolate chips

¼ cup boiling water

¼ cup powdered sugar

3 egg yolks (please see note on eggs, page 9)

½ cup soft butter

2 tablespoons vanilla extract or rum

For a simple and delectable dessert, Dallas Dobosh is hard to beat. A cake that requires no baking, it also looks very elegant, especially when garnished with whipped cream or a few raspberries. The recipe came from my red-headed Dallas friend Diana McDonald, who brought it as the grand finale to a dinner that she served us as a baby gift when our daughter Anna was born. Diana's torte is a good choice to make ahead for a party, as it keeps to perfection for several days, refrigerated. It's splendid with coffee.

USING A LONG SHARP KNIFE, slice the pound cake lengthwise into 6 thin layers (they need not be perfectly even). Keeping them in order for later reassembly, cover them and set them aside.

Chocolate buttercream

To make the buttercream, put the chocolate chips into a blender or food processor with the boiling water. Blend them at high speed for 10 seconds or until the mixture is smooth. Then add the powdered sugar, egg yolks, butter, and vanilla or rum, and blend at high speed until the buttercream is perfectly smooth.

First protecting the serving plate with wax paper, arrange the bottom layer of cake on the plate, spread with buttercream, and put the rest of the layers together in the same way. Frost the top and sides. Then remove the wax paper and refrigerate the cake. Cover it as soon as the frosting is firm, and keep it chilled until serving time.

Cactus Birthday Cake

SERVES 10

1¼ cups sugar

2 tablespoons grated lemon zest

1½ cups (6 ounces) cake flour,
sifted before measuring

½ teaspoon salt

1 teaspoon baking powder

1 cup softened butter

4 eggs

2 teaspoons lemon juice

1½ teaspoons vanilla extract

2 cups powdered
sugar, sieved or sifted

Pinch of salt

2 tablespoons softened butter

Juice of 1 lime

1 teaspoon grated lemon zest

1–3 drops green food coloring

1 drop yellow food coloring

A few drops of milk or water
(optional)

At the end of May, which is peak cactus-blossom season in southern Arizona, I invented this whimsical cake for my daughter Mary's sixteenth birthday. It only looks like a spiny succulent; it's actually a lemon-lime pound cake with a meltingly tender crumb. Like all pound cakes it lasts well, even growing mellower and more flavorful with time.

PREHEAT THE OVEN to 350 degrees F. Grease and flour an 8-cup baking pan with a decorative pattern or vertical flutes that resemble a columnar cactus, such as a baby barrel or a saguaro.

Place the sugar and lemon zest in a blender or food processor and pulse 4 or 5 times to combine them. In a medium bowl whisk together the flour, salt, and baking powder.

Cream the butter in a large mixing bowl and add the sugar and lemon zest, beating until the mixture is very light and fluffy. Add the eggs, lemon juice, and vanilla, followed by the flour mixture in three batches. Beat the batter just until completely smooth, and pour it into the prepared pan, smoothing the top.

Bake at the middle level of the oven at 350 degrees F for 15 minutes, and then turn the heat down to 325 degrees and continue to bake for about 35 minutes more, until the cake is a rich golden brown and a cake tester inserted in the middle comes out clean.

Cool the cake in the pan for about 10 minutes before removing it to a wire rack to cool completely.

Frosting

Cream together the sugar, salt, and butter. Add the lime juice and lemon zest and beat until smooth, adding enough food coloring to tint the frosting pale yellow-green. If necessary, add drops of lime or lemon juice, milk, or water to produce a good spreading consistency.

Frost the cooled cake, smoothing the surface as much as possible. Following the flutes, draw vertical lines in the frosting with the knife or spatula to suggest cactus ribs.

Decoration

- 5 large marshmallows (or 1 per year or per guest)
- Yellow decorating sugar
- Toothpicks
- Small white or yellow birthday candles

Snip the top of each marshmallow several times with kitchen scissors, reaching about halfway down. These cut portions will become petals. Now spread open each marshmallow like a flower and pinch each section gently with your fingers to flatten it, sculpting petals. Be sure to expose the sticky interior of the marshmallow inside each "blossom." Then sprinkle the sticky marshmallow with yellow sugar to resemble cactus pollen.

Attach the flowers to the top of the cake with toothpicks, including at least one blossom per flute. Then position the candles in vertical rows along the flutes to suggest cactus spines, which actually grow in neat patterns, not randomly.

VARIATION This cake can also be baked as a single large loaf in a 5 x 9-inch (8 cup) pan, and instead of decorating it like a cactus, you can top it with this tangy lemon or lemon-lime glaze.

Glaze

½ cup sugar

¼ cup lemon juice, or 2 tablespoons lemon juice and 2 tablespoons lime juice

Begin the glaze when you first remove the cake from the oven. In a small nonreactive saucepan bring the juice and sugar to a boil and stir until the sugar dissolves. Simmer on low heat for a minute or two to thicken the syrup slightly. When the cake has cooled for 10 minutes, turn it out onto the rack and prick the top and sides thoroughly with a toothpick or skewer. Use a pastry brush to apply the warm syrup to all the pricked areas of the cake, and allow it to finish cooling.

El Dorado Chocolate Cake

The Spanish legend of El Dorado—a golden paradise of wealth and abundance—was only a myth. But this cake is a real treasure, flavored with New World chocolate and chile and gilded just before serving with caramel instead of gold. It was adapted from a recipe created by the Tucson artist and musician Cantrell Maryott. In this cake, chile connoisseurs prefer ancho, known as "the sweetie of chile peppers." For sources, see page 11. But any fresh, fragrant, mild to medium-hot chile powder can substitute. Start with a small amount, taste the batter, and adjust the spice to the level you like.

The movie *Chocolat* amusingly dramatizes the seductive taste of chocolate enhanced with ancho chile. But if the idea of "hot" chocolate cake is just too much for you, this recipe makes a fine, moist cake without the ancho chile powder.

SERVES 10

1½ teaspoons ancho chile powder (or up to 3 tablespoons, depending on taste)

1⅓ cups water

2 cups flour

¾ cup cocoa

1¼ teaspoons baking soda

½ teaspoon salt

¾ cup softened butter

1¾ cups sugar

2 eggs

1 teaspoon vanilla extract

PREHEAT THE OVEN to 350 degrees F. Grease, flour, and line with paper 2 cake pans (9-inch).

In a small nonreactive saucepan, simmer the chile powder in the water for 15 minutes, and then let the mixture cool to room temperature. (Cooking enhances the flavor of chile.) Meanwhile put the flour, cocoa, soda, and salt in a medium mixing bowl, and whisk them together.

Next, cream the butter and sugar together in a large mixing bowl until they are very light and fluffy. Add the eggs, one at a time, then add the vanilla, and beat well. Blend in one third of the dry ingredients, followed by half of the cooled chile water. Repeat, and then finish with the last third of the flour mixture.

Pour the batter into the prepared pans, smooth the tops, and bake at the middle level of the oven for 35–40 minutes, or until the cake is lightly springy, and a cake tester inserted in the center comes out clean. When the cake layers are thoroughly cool, frost the cake, and just before you serve it, sprinkle it generously with Caramel Gold Dust (recipe follows).

Three suggested frostings

Seafoam

MAKES ABOUT 3 CUPS

A mellow, brown-sugar variant of seven-minute frosting.

2 egg whites

1½ cups packed brown sugar

Pinch of salt

⅓ cup water

1 teaspoon vanilla extract

COMBINE THE EGG WHITES, sugar, salt, and water in the top of a double boiler, and beat with a portable electric mixer until they are thoroughly mixed. Then place the pan over an inch or two of simmering water, and continue to cook and beat until the frosting is glossy and holds stiff peaks, about 7 minutes. Remove from the heat and add the vanilla; beat thoroughly, and immediately spread on the cake.

MAKES 3½ CUPS

½ cup softened butter

8 ounces cream cheese, softened

Pinch of salt

About 3½ cups (1 pound) powdered sugar, sifted

2–3 tablespoons milk or cream

FLAVOR WITH:

2 teaspoons vanilla extract and ½ teaspoon ground cinnamon, or

Grated zest of 1 orange and 1 tablespoon lemon or orange juice

Cream Cheese Icing

This adds a nice creamy tartness.

IN A LARGE MIXING BOWL, beat the butter and cream cheese together until they are smooth. Gradually add the salt and powdered sugar, beat thoroughly, and then add your choice of liquids and flavorings.

MAKES 2⅔ CUPS

12 ounces bittersweet chocolate (4 bars, 3 ounces each)

1⅔ cups sour cream

¾ teaspoon ground cinnamon (optional)

Chocolate Sour Cream Ganache

This is very lovely and very rich.

ALLOW THE SOUR CREAM to come to room temperature. Then melt the chocolate, either in a microwave at high power, stirring every 10 seconds, or in a double boiler over simmering water. Remove the melted chocolate from the heat and stir in the sour cream and optional cinnamon with a rubber scraper. Use immediately.

Caramel Gold Dust and Caramel Lightning

MAKES ENOUGH DECORATION
FOR 3–4 CAKES, OR ENOUGH
LIGHTNING BOLTS FOR 2 RECIPES
OF CLOUDS IN THE SKY (PAGE 92)

1 cup sugar

⅓ cup water

⅛ teaspoon cream of tartar

To make gold and lightning you need an accurate candy thermometer, a long-handled heatproof spoon, a 2-cup heatproof glass measuring cup, and two baking sheets lined with aluminum foil. Caramel is not difficult to make, but it requires close attention as it cooks to a very high temperature (about 350 degrees F) and can easily boil over, burn, or burn you. Caramel also quickly becomes sticky in humid air, so it should be attempted only on a dry day and then immediately served or stored airtight.

Combine the 3 ingredients in a small, heavy saucepan, and, stirring constantly, cook them over medium heat until the sugar dissolves and the liquid grows clear. Then raise the heat to medium high, clip the candy thermometer to the edge of the pan, and boil without stirring, watching closely, until the temperature reaches 350–360 degrees F and the color reaches a true, rich amber.

Remove from the heat and immediately pour the syrup into the glass measuring cup, where it can be reheated if necessary in a microwave. Cool it slightly, to about 240 degrees, and pour it out onto the foil-lined pans in large irregular shapes for gold dust or 3–4-inch zigzag patterns for lightning bolts.

Caramel hardens almost instantly. When it is cool, carefully remove the lightning bolts, wrap them, and store them airtight until just before serving. They will keep successfully if they are wrapped, frozen flat, and well protected. For gold dust, break the caramel into smaller pieces and pulverize it in a blender or food processor. Store gold dust in a tightly sealed jar in the freezer. Sprinkle it generously over the El Dorado cake just before serving.

Chocolate Lightning

These bolts are easier to make than caramel, especially in humid weather.

MAKES ABOUT 8 BOLTS

½ cup chocolate chips

1 teaspoon vegetable shortening

LAY A SHEET OF WAX PAPER about 12 inches long on a kitchen counter. Melt the chocolate chips with the shortening over low heat or in a microwave, stirring often. When the mixture is completely smooth, use a teaspoon to dribble it onto the wax paper in zigzag shapes 4–6 inches long and about ½ inch thick. To speed up the setting process, refrigerate the chocolate. Just before serving, and working quickly, peel the lightning bolts from the paper and place them upright on the cake or among the clouds (see page 92).

Tres Leches Cake

Pastel de tres leches or "three milks cake" is a recent arrival in the United States from someplace to the south—whether Nicaragua, Guatemala, or Mexico is unclear. The three "milks" that go into this lavish, festive treat are condensed milk, evaporated milk, and heavy cream, which in Latin America is also conveniently available in a can (the Nestlé product, sold as *media crema,* sometimes appears in American specialty stores). That makes every ingredient a pantry staple, even possibly the fruit garnish. Tres Leches Cake is so sweet and rich, and so extremely white, that tart colorful fruits greatly enhance it, especially strawberries. Other delicious possibilities include raspberries, blueberries, blackberries, bananas, peaches, mangos, nectarines, orange sections, and pineapple, or a mixture of these. Although this recipe is less sweet than some Tres Leches Cakes, small servings are completely satisfying.

SERVES 20

1½ cups all-purpose flour

2 teaspoons baking powder

½ teaspoon salt

6 eggs, separated

½ teaspoon cream of tartar

1 cup sugar

⅓ cup cold water

2 teaspoons vanilla extract

1 teaspoon almond extract

LINE A GREASED 9 x 13-inch baking pan with wax paper. Grease and flour the pan, including the paper. Preheat the oven to 350 degrees F.

Whisk together the flour, baking powder, and salt in a medium-sized mixing bowl. In a larger bowl, beat the 6 egg whites until they are foamy. Then add the cream of tartar and continue to whip until soft peaks form.

In another large bowl, beat the egg yolks until they are light and thick. Still beating, gradually add the sugar, and continue whipping until the mixture forms a slowly dissolving ribbon when dripped from the beater. Add the cold water and vanilla and almond extracts to the yolk mixture, followed by the flour mixture. Delicately fold the beaten egg whites into the batter.

Scrape the batter into the prepared pan and smooth the top. Bake the cake for 25–30 minutes, or until its center is lightly springy and a cake tester comes out clean. Allow the cake to cool to room temperature in the pan (about 20 minutes).

Then run a knife around the sides of the pan, cover with a deep serving platter with a lip to contain the three milks, and carefully invert the cake onto the platter. To insure better absorption of the liquid, prick the surface of the cake all over with a fork.

(continued on page 52)

Three Milks

1 14-ounce can condensed milk

1 5-ounce can evaporated milk

1 cup heavy cream (or a 7.6-ounce can Nestlé media crema)

2 teaspoons vanilla extract, or 1 tablespoon rum or brandy

While the cake cools, mix the condensed milk, evaporated milk, cream, and vanilla (or rum or brandy) in a 1-quart measuring pitcher. Pour the liquid bit by bit over the cake, cover it, and refrigerate it for several hours or overnight. Over time, the cake will absorb the three milks, and then it is ready to frost and serve.

Meringue Frosting

4 egg whites

1/8 teaspoon salt

1/4 teaspoon cream of tartar

1/2 cup water

3/4 cup sugar

3 tablespoons light corn syrup

1 teaspoon vanilla extract

In a large mixing bowl or stationary mixer, beat the 4 egg whites with the salt until they are foamy. Then add the cream of tartar and beat until soft peaks form.

Bring the water, sugar, and corn syrup to a boil in a medium-sized saucepan. Cover the pan and boil over medium heat for 2–3 minutes to wash down any sugar crystals from the sides of the pan. Then uncover the pan and continue to boil until the temperature of the sugar syrup reaches 240 degrees F on a candy thermometer, or the soft-ball stage (a few drops will form a malleable shape in a cup of cold water).

Immediately remove the syrup from the heat, begin to beat the egg whites on low speed, and pour the syrup slowly over them. Avoid the beater itself, which will spatter the syrup away from the meringue. When all of the syrup has been added, raise the speed to high and beat the meringue for 2–3 minutes, until it becomes cool and glossy. Blend in the vanilla. Frost the top and sides of the cake, and garnish with fruit just before serving.

Tres Leches Cake will keep well if it is covered and refrigerated for a day or two, either before or after the frosting goes on, so it is a good dessert to make ahead for a special occasion.

Orange-Almond Cake

SERVES 6

½ cup butter

⅔ cup sugar

3 eggs, separated

⅓ cup orange juice, strained

Zest of 1 orange, grated

½ teaspoon almond extract

¾ cup (4 ounces) ground almonds or almond flour

¾ cup (3 ounces) cake flour, sifted before measuring

Pinch of salt

1 tablespoon sugar

Flavorful as it is, this fluffy sponge cake needs no more enhancement than a dusting of powdered sugar or a dollop of whipped or ice cream. It goes very well with fruit and berries, too, and it serves as a base cake for the Grand Canyon Ice Cream Cake (page 113).

GREASE, FLOUR, AND LINE with paper a 9-inch cake pan. Preheat the oven to 350 degrees F.

Melt the butter and set aside to cool slightly. In a large mixing bowl, gradually add ⅔ cup of sugar to the egg yolks, and continue to beat until the mixture is pale yellow and fluffy. Beat in the orange juice, orange zest, and almond extract, followed finally by the ground almonds and the cake flour. Set aside.

Now beat the egg whites and the salt together in a medium mixing bowl until they form soft peaks. Add the tablespoon of sugar, and beat until stiff peaks form.

Fold the tepid butter into the orange batter with a rubber scraper. (Discard the milk solids at the bottom of the melted butter.) Stir about a quarter of the egg whites into the batter, and carefully fold in the rest. Do not overmix.

Fill the prepared cake pan with the batter and smooth the top. Bake in the center of the preheated oven for 30–35 minutes, or until the cake is golden brown and lightly springy to the touch, and a cake tester inserted in the center comes out clean.

Cool the cake in its pan on a wire rack for 10 minutes. Then loosen the edges with a knife and unmold the cake onto the rack. Peel off the paper, turn the cake right-side up, and cool it to room temperature (about an hour). Serve as suggested above.

BREAD TENDS TO BE A SERIOUS SUBJECT, a staff of life and not a treat. The quintessential bread of the West is certainly the tortilla, both corn and wheat, but toothsome as tortillas are, they don't much lend themselves to the frilly nonsense of sweets or desserts. Pioneer biscuits and New Mexican sopaipillas take kindly to honey, as does Native American frybread.

Sweet Breads

In reality, is the serious—even the divine—really ever separate from the comic? "Let me lie down like a stone, O God, and rise up like new bread," murmurs Tolstoy's peasant soldier Platon, in Constance Garnett's translation of *War and Peace*. Then Platon goes off to sleep matter-of-factly among the unspeakable horrors of war, leaving his fellow prisoner, the devastated Pierre, oddly comforted.

These three sweet breads have special ceremonial overtones. Paul's pancakes celebrate the Sonoran Desert saguaro harvest of early summer. In high summer Kim Nelson's zucchini bread takes the squash surplus of the Southwestern kitchen garden and turns it into a long-lasting delicacy. And, in a language of sugar and spice, eggs and oranges, *Pan de Muerto* commemorates the end of harvest, the end of life, and the hope for new joy even on the Day of the Dead.

Better-than-any-other Zucchini Bread

For gardeners struggling with a zucchini population explosion, this is a most valuable recipe. It offers an excellent way to deal with those monster vegetables that sometimes balloon up overnight, although really immense, tough squashes may require peeling, and their massive seeds should be discarded. This is another gem of a recipe from Kim Nelson's *Southwest Kitchen Garden*, handed down from her independent Auntie Vi. Probably Auntie Vi's zucchini bread tastes better than others because it calls for butter instead of vegetable oil, and because the amount of cinnamon is exactly right.

According to my daughter Mary, this is the only good way to use zucchini, except for compost.

MAKES 2 LOAVES, 8 X 4 INCHES EACH

3 eggs

2 cups sugar

⅔ cup butter, melted and cooled

2 cups grated zucchini

2 cups flour

¼ teaspoon baking powder

½ teaspoon baking soda

I tablespoon cinnamon

¼ teaspoon salt

2 teaspoons vanilla extract

I cup chopped pecans or walnuts (optional)

GREASE AND FLOUR the loaf pans and line each one with paper. Preheat the oven to 350 degrees F.

In a large mixing bowl, beat the eggs until they are light and fluffy. Then add the sugar, beat well, and add the melted butter. Mix well, and finally stir in the grated zucchini.

Whisk the flour, baking powder, baking soda, cinnamon, and salt together in a medium mixing bowl. Stir this into the first mixture. When the two are well blended, stir in the vanilla and nuts.

Divide the batter between the two prepared pans. Bake the bread at the middle level of the oven for 1 hour, or until a cake tester inserted in the center of a loaf comes out clean.

Cool the loaves in their pans for 10 minutes. Then unmold them onto wire racks and allow them to cool completely before serving. Zucchini bread is long-lasting at room temperature, if carefully wrapped, and it also freezes well. It makes a good addition to a brown-bag lunch or a picnic basket.

Pan de Muerto (Bread of the Dead)

In Mexico, my birthplace, the big autumn festival is not Halloween night but the Day of the Dead, or *el Día de los Muertos*, which is celebrated technically on November 2, All Soul's Day. But actually the festivities begin on October 31, when the baby spirits start to arrive, and continue for several days and nights. I have a special fondness for both holidays since my late-October birthday falls in that season. My mother remembers that the hospital in Chihuahua where I was born was full of chrysanthemums, one of the traditional flowers of the Day of the Dead.

If American Halloween tastes of pumpkin and trick-or-treat candy, the Day of the Dead tastes of tamales and chocolate-chile mole sauce (meals are served both at home and in graveyards to both the living and the departed family members). Sweets are important, too, for it is well known that the dead love sugar, especially the littlest *angelitos.* And sugar takes many forms, including colorful sugar skulls personalized with the names of the quick and the dead, and many loaves of this handsome bread. Like the holiday, the bread blends European with Native American traditions, all of which probably predate the Christian era. Since warming or toasting enhances its delicate anise and orange flavors, Pan de Muerto makes a splendid breakfast bread, and accompanied by a frothy cup of Mexican hot chocolate (see page 79), it's sublime. It freezes well, though you might want to sprinkle on a fresh coat of sugar before serving. The coarser crystals of decorating sugar retain their shape better than table sugar.

**MAKES 2 ROUND LOAVES, EACH
6–7 INCHES IN DIAMETER**

½ cup butter

½ cup milk

½ cup water

5–5½ cups flour

2 packages (4½ teaspoons)
dry yeast

2 teaspoons salt

1 tablespoon anise seed

½ cup sugar

4 eggs, room temperature

FOR DECORATION:

2–4 tablespoons coarse
decorating sugar, either
clear or colored

HEAT THE BUTTER, milk, and water together in a small saucepan (or in a microwave) until they are very warm. The butter need not completely melt. Set aside.

In a large mixing bowl, blend together 1½ cups of flour with the yeast, salt, anise seed, and sugar. Using a large spoon, beat in the warm milk mixture to make a soft batter. One by one, add the eggs and another cup of flour. Continue adding flour until the dough becomes too stiff to stir. Then either finish kneading with the dough hook attachment of an electric mixer or by hand on a lightly floured board. (Be sparing with the flour; too much will make bread dry.) In 5–10 minutes the dough will become velvety smooth and elastic.

Then form it into a ball, and let it rise for 1–2 hours in a buttered bowl in a warm place, covered with a clean towel or a sheet of plastic wrap, until the dough has doubled in size. Punch it down, and divide it into three equal parts. Divide one of these parts in two. Now shape each of the larger portions into a round ball by tucking the edges underneath and pinching them to seal the bottoms. Place each loaf on a greased baking sheet.

Pinch off about a fifth of each of the smaller portions and shape two small balls. These are sometimes called *lágrimas* (tears) and sometimes *suspiros* (sighs). Poke a small hole in the top of each big ball of dough with your finger, pinch and taper one side of each lágrima into a teardrop shape, and insert the thinner end into the top of the big ball, pinching lightly to seal. Then divide the remaining dough into 8 small pieces and roll each one out into a cylindrical *hueso* or bone, sometimes also called a lágrima. These long pieces are often thinned by extra rolling in the middle or at one end, depending on whether you see them as a bones or tears.

Moisten them slightly with water and attach four of them in a crossbone pattern starting at the top and wrapping the sides of each loaf, pinching gently to make them stick close to the central sigh or teardrop. (Alternatively, the dough may be sculpted into skull, ghost, or skeleton shapes, or many smaller loaves.) Cover the loaves with towels or plastic and let them rise until double, about 1 hour.

While the dough rises, make the glaze (recipe follows).

Preheat the oven to 350 degrees F. Bake the risen Pan de Muerto for 30–40 minutes, reversing the pans at the halfway point. Remove when the loaves are well-browned and sound hollow when tapped on the bottom. Using a pastry brush, paint each loaf with glaze and immediately sprinkle them with decorating sugar.

Glaze

⅓ cup sugar
¼ cup orange juice
4 teaspoons grated orange zest

In a small nonreactive saucepan, simmer these ingredients for 2 minutes. Set aside until the bread is baked.

Cactus Pancakes

This recipe is easy to remember and excellent either with or without cactus. It comes from two Arizona artists, Paul Mirocha and Rhod Lauffer, who worked together to make the extraordinary origami illustrations for my children's novel *The Boy with Paper Wings*. Rhod's Kentucky heritage provided the mnemonic pancake recipe (all the measurements come in 1s or 2s), which Paul adapted for summer pancake breakfasts he often gives for a large group of friends to commemorate the traditional saguaro-cactus harvest in late May or early June. "We all get up early and pick the fruit," says Paul, "then have the breakfast as soon as we get home."

Picking the fruit involves knocking it down from the tops of giant cacti with special harvesting sticks. The fruit itself tastes like a cross between strawberries and figs, only better. (See the recipe for saguaro sundaes on page 109.) Paul's simplified recipe for cactus syrup: "Scrape the pulp out of the fruit. Boil half of it down into syrup and leave the rest raw. Some boiled-down syrup is mixed with the batter but also is great mixed with a little real maple syrup and put on the pancakes. The raw cactus fruit is also great, depending on personal tastes, but we also add other kinds of fresh fruit, sliced on top of the fresh pancakes."

MAKES ABOUT 16 PANCAKES

2 cups flour

2 teaspoons baking powder

½ teaspoon salt

2 tablespoons sugar (optional if adding sweet syrup)

2 cups milk

2 eggs

½ stick (¼ cup) melted butter or margarine

Saguaro or prickly pear pulp and/or syrup to taste (other fruit pulp and/or syrup, such as strawberry, raspberry, or boysenberry, can substitute)

WHISK TOGETHER the flour, baking powder, salt, and sugar in a medium mixing bowl. In a separate small bowl, beat together the milk and eggs. Add the wet ingredients to the dry ones, mix well, and blend in the melted butter. Add saguaro syrup (and pulp) till you like the color, or substitute prickly pear or other fruit products.

Using a hot, greased griddle or skillet, cook the pancakes until they are lightly browned on both sides, and for best results, turn them only once. Tricky shapes may need to be flipped with a pair of pancake turners.

PAUL'S VARIATION WHEN KIDS ARE INVITED Add chocolate chips or candies to the batter, and provide a variety of sliced fruits to make faces on the pancakes before eating. "We also make rabbit-shaped pancakes," says Paul, "or saguaros, desert animals, or anything…"

CONFECTIONS ARE GENERALLY SUGARY, but I have included prickly pear fruit leather and roasted pecans in this collection. Since they are less sweet, they offer an excellent contrast in a holiday gift box or on a candy tray. The pecans are a particularly luscious local treat in the pecan-growing regions of the West, and the prickly pear fruit strips are both regional and healthful.

Small Confections

Toffee

Candy has many entertaining names, such as heavenly hash, lollipops, and fudge. What's the difference between taffy and toffee? Is this superlative stuff really toffee, or should it be labeled "almond butter crunch"? I learned to make it by eye and by taste, and I have always regarded it as a kind of magical preparation, so you will not find thermometer readings or a scientific explanation for the mysterious but harmless butter-separation phenomenon. Nor can I explain why this recipe requires salted butter. I do know that toffee is impossible to make in summer, or at other times of high humidity, perhaps because then the sugar will not caramelize properly. But really toffee should be made only in limited quantities around the time of the winter solstice. Otherwise, it's like leaving the Christmas tree up too long.

I received this recipe from my friend Ardith Arnold many Christmases ago, and Ardith calls it toffee. An Irish acquaintance calls it "simply scroomy." Beware! Toffee makes people pursue you until the toffee vanishes, and then they will want the recipe.

MAKES ABOUT 2½ POUNDS

I pound butter (salted)

2 cups sugar

I cup almonds (slivered, sliced, or whole; either blanched or unblanched)

Water as necessary

8 ounces chocolate (milk chocolate bars, semisweet, or finest bittersweet)

½ cup toasted pecans, very finely chopped

SET OUT a 10 x 15-inch nonstick baking sheet or an equivalent sheet of aluminum foil on a heatproof surface. In a large, heavy saucepan (at least 4-quart) over medium heat, bring the butter to the boiling point. Add the sugar, stirring with a long-handled wooden or heatproof spoon, until this mixture begins to boil. Then add the almonds, bring the candy to a boil again, and continue to boil and stir over medium heat for 15–20 minutes or more. If possible, recruit someone to help you stir.

Very often during the cooking process several tablespoons of butter, or even more, will separate from the candy and float on top. When this happens, add 2–4 tablespoons of water and stir, being careful of the steam, which is extremely hot. The water will force the candy to re-absorb the butter, although it will lower the temperature and slow down the cooking. You may have to repeat this process several times, but by the time the toffee is done the butter will stop separating.

Gradually the candy will turn from pale yellow to medium golden brown. After 12 minutes, begin to test it by spreading out a tablespoonful with a metal spoon as thinly as possible on a cool plate. Remove the pot from the heat while you are testing, or the toffee may burn. Before the candy is ready, the texture will appear sugary and soft; then it will grow harder and browner, and finally it will become crisp.

Key signs of doneness: the almonds are thoroughly toasted, the color is a mellow brown, and the texture is smooth, appearing almost melted. When it is stirred vigorously, the toffee will clump into a heavy wreath. And a spoonful will spread very thin and crunch when bitten.

As soon as it is done, immediately pour the toffee out onto the baking sheet, and spread it to an even thickness, if necessary. Be careful not to burn yourself. Unwrap the chocolate, break it into squares, and distribute them evenly over the hot candy. Within a few minutes they will melt. Spread the chocolate to cover the top of the toffee, and sprinkle it evenly with chopped pecans. Allow it to cool for several hours or overnight. When the chocolate is set and the toffee is thoroughly cool, break it into bite-sized pieces and store it airtight.

NOTE To clean the saucepan and spoon, fill pan with hot, soapy water and let them soak. The candy will rapidly melt away.

Famous Fudge

MAKES ABOUT 4½ POUNDS

4 cups sugar

I can (12 ounces) evaporated milk

I cup butter

¼ teaspoon salt

4 ounces or 20 large marshmallows, snipped in half, or 2 cups mini-marshmallows

18 ounces semisweet chocolate chips

2 teaspoons vanilla extract

2 cups chopped nuts, any kind (optional)

2 cups mini-marshmallows (optional)

Is this the actual fudge recipe used by See's, the famous Western candy company? Is it the only See's recipe not kept secret? Whatever the truth of the matter may be, here's a delectable and foolproof formula for chocolate fudge. It also produces a huge quantity of candy, but it works equally well when all ingredients are halved.

In New Mexico, piñon nuts are a favorite addition to fudge, and mini-marshmallows will transform it into Rocky Road fudge.

BUTTER ONE LARGE (15 x 13-inch or 13 x 9-inch) or two smaller (11 x 7-inch or 8 x 8-inch) pans.

In a large (at least 4-quart), deep saucepan bring the sugar, evaporated milk, butter, and salt to a rolling boil, and continue to boil this mixture for 8 minutes. Then remove it from the heat, add the marshmallows and chocolate chips, and stir vigorously with a heavy spoon until they melt and the candy is uniform in texture. Stir in the vanilla and the optional nuts or mini-marshmallows.

Scrape the fudge into the pan or pans. Refrigerate for 24 hours before serving. Closely covered, this candy keeps very well for months in the refrigerator.

Roasted Pecans

Dick and Nan Stockholm Walden live among the groves of their Green Valley Pecan Company near Green Valley, Arizona. They often serve these delectable toasted nuts to dinner guests before, during, and after a meal. A few roasted pecans make a lovely non-sweet dessert all by themselves, and they also combine well with coffee. As the Waldens point out, pecans offer many nutritional benefits along with their rich taste.

MAKES 1 CUP

1–2 tablespoons butter

I cup fresh pecan halves

Salt

IN A HEAVY SKILLET over medium-low heat, melt the butter and add the pecan halves. Continue to heat them, stirring occasionally, for 5–10 minutes, until they are evenly roasted and fragrant. Sprinkle with salt and serve.

For larger quantities, it's easier to put the nuts and butter on a rimmed baking sheet and bake them in a 300-degree oven, stirring frequently, for 5–10 minutes, or until nicely brown. Sprinkle with salt and serve.

Popcorn Nuggets

MAKES ABOUT 10 CUPS

2 quarts popped, salted corn
(about ½ cup unpopped)

1 cup roasted, salted almonds
(blanched or not)

1 cup roasted, salted pecans
(or cashews, or half of each)

1⅓ cups sugar

½ cup light corn syrup

1 cup butter

Popcorn is a very old treat; archaeologists have discovered prehistoric kernels of it preserved in ancient pueblos. Of course it's good plain and hot. But undoubtedly the best popcorn I know is this golden caramel corn mixed with freshly toasted nuts. Appropriately enough, it comes from the star-studded recipe files of my neighbor Ardith Arnold, a native of Midwestern corn country.

MIX THE POPCORN and nuts in a large shallow pan.

In a heavy 1½-quart saucepan bring the sugar, corn syrup, and butter to a boil. Clip a candy thermometer to the side of the pan and continue boiling for 10–15 minutes, or until the caramel turns light brown and reaches a point between soft and hard crack (280–300 degrees F). Pour this syrup over the popcorn and nuts. Mix well and spread the popcorn out to cool. Then break into bite-sized nuggets and store it in a covered container. (It will keep well only if the cover stays on!)

Chocolate Popcorn

MAKES ABOUT 5½ CUPS, OR 8–10 SMALL POPCORN BALLS

5 cups popped corn

3 ounces unsweetened chocolate

1 cup sugar

½ cup water

⅓ cup light corn syrup

3 tablespoons butter

Is it popcorn? Or is it fudge? This confection passed along from Ardith's mother, Mildred Propst, is richer than the first, lighter than the second, and it makes wonderful popcorn balls. In the days of rationing during World War II, Mrs. Propst used this recipe as a way to stretch her precious candy ingredients.

PLACE THE POPCORN in a large mixing bowl.

In a large heavy saucepan over very low heat, melt the chocolate. Add the sugar, water, corn syrup, and butter, and bring the mixture to a boil over medium heat. Clip a candy thermometer to the side of the pan, and cook the fudge to the hard ball stage (254 degrees F). Pour it slowly over the popcorn in the bowl, and quickly mix everything together.

At this point you can butter your hands and make popcorn balls, or you can simply spread the chocolate popcorn on a buttered cookie sheet, sheets of parchment, or wax paper. Break it into bite-sized pieces when it cools, and store it in an airtight container. Popcorn balls should be wrapped airtight, too.

Prickly Pear Fruit Strips

MAKES ABOUT 48 STRIPS OR
ROLLS, 1 INCH EACH

About 35 ripe, plump prickly
pear fruits (8–10 fruits yield
about 1 cup of juice)

Water as necessary

4 teaspoons honey

6 ounces grape juice concentrate

This recipe comes from Wayne Peate's inspiring *Native Healing: Four Sacred Paths to Health*. As Dr. Peate points out, native foods such as cactus contain many health benefits that we are only beginning to understand. You may substitute 4 cups of bottled, unsweetened prickly pear nectar for the 4 cups of juice yielded by the ripe fruits and water listed below.

USING TONGS, pick the prickly pear fruits, place them in a large plastic container, rinse, drain, and freeze them. Then allow them to defrost. Press them with a potato masher, or whirl them in a blender about 6 at a time, adding a little water if necessary. Then pour the "purple mess," as Dr. Peate describes it, through a colander lined with several thicknesses of cheesecloth. You should have about 4 cups of prickly pear juice.

Mix prickly pear juice or nectar with the honey and grape juice concentrate. Spread the mixture on 4 baking sheets covered with plastic wrap. Dry it in an oven at the lowest setting; this can take all day. After the fruit leather is dry, peel the plastic off, roll the fruit up in strips, and cut into bite-size pieces. "And enjoy," says Dr. Peate.

IN ANCIENT TIMES, dessert was not an elaborate pastry but a light, refreshing fruit course, served after the main meal was done. In fact, the original meaning of the word "dessert" comes from the idea of "de-" or "un-serving" the table. And fruit treats, such as sliced oranges drizzled with wildflower honey or pears with brown sugar, remain one of the most satisfying ways to "de-serve" that I know.

Originally I planned to call this book *Desert Desserts,* but that quickly created a spelling nightmare. And besides, most Western terrain is not desert at all. Fruits that flourish in Western climates include apples, peaches, apricots, plums, grapes, berries, oranges, grapefruit, and lemons, as well as specialties such as pomegranates, figs, *zapotes* (or sapodillas), quinces, and cactus fruit. This colorful collection of true desserts hits many light and refreshing notes, with only a few hints of refined sugar or fat.

Fruit Desserts

Pomegranate Seeds in White Wine

Judy England was born Juliet Kibbey in Nogales, Arizona, about 1916, soon after the territory became a state, but she was partly raised in Mexico. Her father, an aristocratic Yankee, had built a castle on a hill at the Hacienda el Alamo in northern Sonora, where Judy and her sister attended the local one-room school, followed in due course by Bryn Mawr. According to Judy, this was a favorite dessert at the Hacienda el Alamo during the Roaring Twenties.

⅓ cup ripe, red
pomegranate seeds

I glass white
wine, still or sparkling

Sugar to taste (optional)

CUT OR BREAK OPEN a pomegranate. Submerge it in a bowl of cool water, and separate the seeds from the white pith and inedible peel under water. The seeds will sink to the bottom, and the pith will float to the top. Skim it off, and drain the seeds.

Place about ⅓ cup of seeds in the bottom of a pretty wineglass. Fill with wine, sweeten to taste (or not), and serve. If you wish, crush the seeds with a spoon to release pomegranate juice into the wine, or drink the wine and then eat the seeds. One large pomegranate makes 3–4 servings.

Rancho Poco Toro Chuck Wagon Pears

SERVES 6

3 tablespoons butter
or margarine

½ cup brown sugar

½ teaspoon ground cinnamon

¼ teaspoon ground ginger
(optional)

I large can pear halves (I pound
13 ounces)

Cream or vanilla ice cream
(optional but good)

Margie Buyer, of the Rancho Poco Toro near Patagonia, Arizona, frequently cooks wonderful chuck wagon meals. She served these pears to huge acclaim at a gala on the nearby Empire Ranch, now part of the Las Cienegas National Conservation Area. This recipe is highly flexible and easy to cook outdoors in a Dutch oven or heavy skillet over a fire. Allowing two pear halves per person, it can be reduced to serve one, or expanded to serve hundreds.

MELT THE BUTTER in the skillet, and add the brown sugar, cinnamon, and optional ginger. Stir the mixture over low heat until well blended, and then add the pears, drained of their syrup. Simmer them over low heat for about 10 minutes, and serve warm, topped with a few tablespoons of cream or a scoop of ice cream. (Homemade ice cream is the crème de la crème, Margie says.)

Orange Slices with Honey

Oranges—"the golden apples of the sun" in Yeats's lovely phrase—remind me of Christmas. This is partly because there was usually a plump one in the toe of my stocking, and partly because in the warm parts of the West, including Texas, Arizona, and Southern California, oranges ripen around that time. So Christmas visits to my grandmother's ranch at Red Rock, Arizona, often included time spent picking oranges and carrying them home by the dozen in brown grocery bags. I liked to rustle around in the glossy, aromatic green leaves of her huge orange tree, which sometimes bore fruit and flowers at the same time. I never had the same friendly feeling toward her equally gigantic and leafy grapefruit tree, and grapefruit is still too bitter for me.

Vibrant to the eye and the tongue, oranges make a refreshing dessert after a spicy meal. This recipe dresses them up just slightly and is especially good with local or unusual honey. I like to use the wildflower honey that we get as rent from the beekeeper at our Palo Alto Ranch.

SERVES 4

¼ cup honey

4 teaspoons water

2 cinnamon sticks, or
¼ teaspoon ground cinnamon

4 large or 6 small navel oranges

IN A TINY SAUCEPAN, mix the honey with the water and ground cinnamon or cinnamon sticks. Warm it for 5 minutes over very low heat, stirring, but do not let it boil. Set it aside till serving time.

Peel and horizontally slice the oranges, removing as much pithy material as you can, as well as any seeds. Arrange the slices decoratively on serving plates or bowls. Drizzle the oranges with the tepid honey just before serving, and garnish with additional cinnamon sticks, if you like.

Green Grapes with Sour Cream

SERVES 6

6 cups seedless grapes

1 cup sour cream

½–1 cup brown sugar

An unlikely combination? Try it, and see how beautifully the tang and softness of the cream mingle with the sour grape skin and juicy grape pulp. The crumbly, melting brown sugar adds both texture and a flash of molasses sweetness. This exquisite summer dessert originated with Peg Gould, the wife of an Antarctic explorer, who gave it to her friend Ardith Arnold, who gave it to me. (And the grapes can be red as well as green.)

FINGER-FOOD VERSION Divide the grapes into attractive clusters. Wash and gently blot them dry, and arrange them on 6 serving plates or on a single serving platter. Pass the sour cream and brown sugar separately, so that each guest can dip grapes first in a portion of sour cream and then in brown sugar to taste.

SPOON VERSION (RICHER AND POSSIBLY NEATER) Pull the grapes from their stems. Wash and dry them completely by spreading them on a terrycloth kitchen towel and gently rolling them around with a second towel. Place the loose, dry grapes in a serving bowl, and toss them with the sour cream until they are completely covered. Divide the creamy grapes into separate bowls for serving, and pass brown sugar to be sprinkled on top.

Mixed Fruit in Prickly Pear Syrup

SERVES 6

⅓ cup sugar

½ cup water

1 cinnamon stick, or
¼ teaspoon ground cinnamon

1 large sprig fresh mint (optional)

3 tablespoons prickly pear syrup

1 teaspoon vanilla extract

1 large, ripe mango or
peach, peeled and cut in
bite-sized pieces

1½ cups bite-sized pieces
fresh pineapple

3 cups mixed fresh berries, such
as strawberries, blueberries,
blackberries, or raspberries

Fresh mint sprigs for garnish
(optional)

Properly handled, the ripe fruits of the prickly pear cactus can be turned into gorgeous juice, jelly, and syrup—as well as many other delicious recipes to be found in Carolyn Niethammer's *Prickly Pear Cookbook*, which gives detailed instructions for harvesting cactus and extracting the juice. If prickly pear is out of season, or if you lack time, opportunity, or true grit, I recommend the excellent commercial syrups. (See the suppliers listed on page 10.)

Vivid colors make this dessert a highly visual treat.

IN A SMALL SAUCEPAN mix the sugar and water and bring to a boil, stirring until the sugar dissolves and the liquid is clear. Add the cinnamon, mint, prickly pear syrup, and vanilla, stir, and remove from the heat. Allow this mixture to cool and the flavors to blend while you prepare the fruit.

Gently mix the mango or peach and pineapple pieces in a large bowl, catching as much juice as possible. Divide these fruits, followed by the berries, among six glass serving dishes. Remove the cinnamon stick and mint from the prickly pear syrup. Top the bowls of fruit with equal portions of syrup, and garnish each serving with a mint sprig. Serve cold.

Strawberry Mousse

SERVES 6

2 envelopes (½ ounce each) unflavored gelatin

½ cup cold water

2 cups strawberry puree (from 10 ounces strawberries)

2 cups plain yogurt (not nonfat)

⅓ cup sugar, plus more to taste if necessary

Oil in a spray bottle, or unflavored cooking spray

This very pretty recipe comes from *Secrets of Light Latin Cooking*, an elegant, innovative cookbook by three health-conscious Mexico City chefs. For a light and healthful Valentine's Day treat, mold Strawberry Mousse in heart shapes.

IN A TINY SAUCEPAN, soak the gelatin in the cold water for 10 minutes. Then warm it slowly over low heat, and strain it into a small bowl. (This will prevent the formation of gelatin lumps.)

In a blender or food processor, puree the strawberries. Then add the yogurt, sugar, and strained gelatin, and blend until well mixed. Taste, and add more sugar if needed, depending on the sweetness of the berries.

Spray a 1-quart gelatin mold or 6 molds or ramekins (6-ounce) with oil. Pour the strawberry mixture into the mold or molds, cover, and refrigerate until set (2–3 hours).

To unmold, first loosen the top edges of the mousse with your thumbs or a knife blade. Next, either dip the mold briefly in hot water or wrap it in a hot wet towel, and then reverse it quickly over a serving plate.

This delicate pudding is excellent served with sliced fresh strawberries or strawberry sauce, or both. (To make the sauce, simply puree sliced strawberries with sugar to taste.) Mixed berries also work well as a garnish.

VARIATION Pureed mango makes a tangy tropical substitute for strawberries in the mousse.

Fruit Packages

SERVES 6

2 squares (12-inches each) aluminum foil

1 mango or 1 large peach, peeled, seeded, and sliced, or 1 cup frozen, unsweetened peach slices

1 tart green apple, peeled, cored, and sliced

1½ cups frozen, unsweetened cherries

¼ teaspoon cinnamon

2 tablespoons orange juice

2 tablespoons honey (or more to taste)

2 whole cloves

These are an easy fruit treat, especially nice in winter, when you can take advantage of high-quality frozen peaches and cherries. The original version of this recipe, found in *Secrets of Light Latin Cooking*, calls for strawberries instead of cherries, but I think cherries hold their shape, flavor, and color better through the baking.

PREHEAT THE OVEN to 350 degrees F. Distribute equal portions of the fruit between the two foil squares, and sprinkle the fruit with the cinnamon, orange juice, and honey to taste. Add 1 clove to each portion.

Seal the foil tightly into packets, and place them on a rimmed baking sheet. Bake for 20–30 minutes, depending on the degree of crispness you want, and serve the fruit wrapped in the foil packets to catch all the cooking juices. Garnish with whipped cream or ice cream, if desired.

Beverages

EAST OR WEST, the elixir of life and the nectar of the gods must be water. "Cool, clear water," crooned the Sons of the Pioneers in their hit song of 1941—but tepid canteen water can taste utterly ambrosial. A canteen of drinking water was an essential feature of every journey in my childhood; sometimes it consisted of a brown burlap water bag hung on the hood of the car to cool in the breeze. In the desert nobody with any sense goes anywhere without water. Many a grave in a remote Tohono O'odham cemetery in Arizona or in Sonora, Mexico, bears its jar of water—or its baby bottle—along with its flowers and its wooden cross. No grass.

Water doesn't have to be clear, either. Danny Lopez, a Tohono O'odham elder and teacher, once showed a group of his students the *charco* or water hole that he used as a boy before wells were drilled on the reservation. "You *drank* that stuff?" asked the children incredulously. "That's why I'm here," Danny said.

It can even be noxious. In the early twentieth century a bus, or rather a shabby touring car, used to travel the route across the Sonoran Desert just south of the international border, which is still called, with good reason, the *Camino del Diablo,* or Devil's Road. To keep his passengers from getting too greedy, the driver laced the scanty water supply with gasoline.

Fortunately, there are much better ways to flavor water. Here are four especially characteristic cool beverages, which would make perfect refreshments for a celebration of San Juan's Day on a hot, dry June 24. As the feast day of John the Baptist, San Juan's Day supposedly brings the first summer rain to the Southwest, and even just the hope of it is somehow inspiring.

And for the opposite extreme of the calendar, nothing could possibly surpass a foamy, steamy cup of Mexican hot chocolate on a cold winter morning.

Juanita Punch

MAKES ABOUT 20
SERVINGS, ½ CUP EACH

1 12-ounce can frozen
limeade concentrate

1 10-ounce can frozen
margarita-mix concentrate

2 cups cold water

1 liter (approximately
4 cups) Squirt or other
mixed-citrus soda

Ice

Salt

Lime slices or wedges
(optional)

"Juanita is Margarita's little sister," explains Janice Johnson, who created this pale green sparkling punch recipe. "She is too young to go out with Jose Cuervo."

Janice, owner of the Hilltop Gallery in Nogales, Arizona, adds: "I made up the punch story because we live on a high hilltop and people need to be refreshed and in full control to get down the hill!"

Suitable for all ages, Juanita Punch adds innocent, thirst-quenching zest to a barbecue, Mexican buffet, or New Year's Eve party.

IN A PUNCH BOWL, combine the limeade and margarita-mix concentrates with the water and Squirt, and add about half as much ice as you have punch. If you like, squeeze a fresh lime or two into the mixture. Then sprinkle the punch lightly with salt, and add more to taste, if necessary. For an elegant touch, rub the punch cups or glasses with lime juice, rim with salt, and serve garnished with lime.

Pink Javelina Punch

MAKES ABOUT 20 SERVINGS, ½ CUP EACH

2 liters (approximately 2 quarts) ginger ale

2 cups cranberry-raspberry juice, or to taste

Juice of 3 fresh limes

Ice

This sparkling refreshment was invented by my good friend John Heider—a great connoisseur of books as well as food—to serve at book signings for *The Three Little Javelinas* when it first came out in 1992. I am sure that javelinas would enjoy it too, since as far as I know they happily eat or drink absolutely anything.

IN A PUNCH BOWL, combine the ginger ale, cranberry-raspberry juice, and lime juice, and stir. Add about half as much ice as the volume of punch, and serve.

PECCARY PUNCH (AN ADULT VARIATION) To 1 batch Pink Javelina Punch, add 1 cup vodka.

Sun Tea

Sun
Water
Tea
Time
That's all there is to it.

I used to make huge jars of sun tea. It was very, very easy on a sizzling summer day, and I loved to watch as hour by hour the wave of amber tea crept into the clear water. But then my vats of tea would languish in the refrigerator, slowly growing bitter and cloudy. So now I make it by the glass, or glasses, instead of by the gallon. It's just as beautiful as it brews, and sun tea, like many other simple foods, tastes best fresh.

SERVES 1

1 tea bag (or infuser filled with loose tea)

1 cup water (filtered or bottled, if desired)

POUR THE WATER into a transparent drinking glass that will hold at least 12 ounces (leaving room for ice). Add the tea bag or tea infuser. With tea as with water, it helps to pay attention to quality. Many different types and flavors of tea are good cold, including most herb teas.

Cover the glass or glasses with plastic wrap, and place the future tea in bright sunlight, either indoors or outside, for a minimum of 1 hour and possibly much longer, depending on the strength you prefer. Flavor is more important than color here, so the tea maker should always taste before serving. And without a real blast of sun, the water will turn brown, but the flavor won't develop.

VARIATION Steep a sprig of mint or a cinnamon stick in the water along with the tea.

Prickly Pear Lemonade

SERVES 4

4 or 5 lemons

6 cups water

¼ to ½ cup sugar

¼ cup prickly pear syrup

Ice

Sprigs of mint and fresh lemon slices (optional)

We played a game called Making Lemonade on the playground of Lincoln School in Prescott, Arizona, when I was six or seven. It was a variation of charades in which one child acted out a process while the others guessed what it was. Once I pretended to make lemonade, but nobody guessed it, and I grew very weary of squeezing imaginary lemons before we moved on to other games, such as the often terrifying Red Rover.

This formula is slightly adapted from Carolyn Niethammer's spectacular lemonade recipe in *The Prickly Pear Cookbook*. There's abundant lemon flavor from the cut rind—and no squeezing. It reminds me of a vendor who used to peddle drinks at University of Arizona football games by bellowing up and down the stadium: "Ice-cold lemonade! *Limonada!* It's—so—LEMONY!"

SCRUB THE LEMONS and slice them ¼ inch thick. Place them in a large heatproof bowl or pitcher. Bring the water to a boil, pour it over the lemons, and stir in the sugar. Let the lemonade steep for 4 hours, strain off the juice, and add the prickly pear syrup. Taste and correct for sweetness. Then either refrigerate, or serve immediately over ice, garnished with mint and lemon slices if you like.

LAZY SHORTCUT VARIATION Add fresh lemon slices and prickly pear syrup to lemonade made from commercial frozen concentrate.

Mexican Hot Chocolate

When you look past the froth and into the depths of a cup of Mexican chocolate, and you breathe in the warm fragrance, you get just a whiff of a lost world, for pre-Columbian chocolate drinks were unsweetened and probably laced with herbs, spices, and chile. Still, the invading Spaniards immediately took to chocolatl, mixing it with sugar, cinnamon, and sometimes ground almonds to make an extremely good drink.

In the beginning, chocolate was only for drinking, never for eating or baking. Technological refinements made chocolate cake and candy possible, but only quite recently. In modern Mexico and places with long ties to it, like the American West, drinking chocolate (which actually doesn't work well in baking) comes to market in fat, rough brown disks packaged under brand names such as Ibarra or Abuelita. This is a very lightly processed product, still quite close to the cacao bean and to the primeval chocolatl. Before it will blend successfully with hot liquid it must be whipped. In Mexico the traditional tool for this is a wooden beater called a *molinillo*, which cooks roll rapidly between their palms. Also traditional is a chocolate nursery rhyme, which you recite as you beat, faster and faster:

¡Uno, dos, tres, CHO! One, two, three, CHO!
¡Uno, dos, tres, CO! One, two, three, CO!
¡Uno, dos, tres, LA! One, two, three, LA!
¡Uno, dos, tres, TE! One, two, three, TE!
[Accelerate the pace.]
¡Chocolate, chocolate, Chocolate, chocolate,
Bate, bate, chocolate! Beat, beat, chocolate!
¡Bate, bate, bate, bate, Beat, beat, beat, beat,
Bate, bate, CHOCOLATE! Beat, beat, CHOCOLATE!

SERVES 1

1 cup milk (or water, for chocolate purists)

1–1½ ounces Mexican chocolate, coarsely chopped

IN A DEEP SAUCEPAN stir the milk or water and chocolate over medium heat until the mixture is steaming and the chocolate is mostly melted. Then either transfer to a blender and blend to a smooth, foamy texture, or whip it well in the pan with a whisk or immersion blender. Serve hot (you may have to reheat it).

Don't forget the rhyme.

Puddings

"PUDDING—ALICE; ALICE—PUDDING."

In the flip-flopped world on the far side of Lewis Carroll's looking glass, the Red Queen introduces Alice to her dessert. But since "it isn't etiquette to cut any one you've been introduced to," the queen then cries, to Alice's dismay: "Remove the pudding!"

"Pudding" is to the British what "dessert" is to Americans. The word has various meanings, ranging from a soft and spongy cream to a very heavy concoction boiled in a bag, like Alice's plum pudding, which speaks up indignantly in a "thick, suety sort of voice." Puddings are an amorphous and adaptable species, sometimes baked, sometimes boiled, and hard to ruin.

This is possible, however. Working as a cowboy on a ranch in Kansas around 1880, my homesick English great-grandfather once attempted to make a plum pudding like Alice's. But he lacked some key ingredient—surely not suet, perhaps dried fruit—and his pudding was a dreadful failure. Although he tried to throw it away, the ghastly mess continued to haunt him, for the ranch dogs retrieved it from the dump and spent weeks gleefully rolling the petrified pudding round and round the barnyard like a bowling ball, or maybe the utterly indigestible Ghost of Christmas Past.

The puddings that follow are all members of the tender, friendly group, so please do not allow yourself to be formally introduced to any of them.

Natillas

Late on a summer afternoon in northern New Mexico, sunlight filled the old San Rafael church. Sky-blue paint reached only halfway across the new wooden ceiling, but the workers' scaffolding had been moved for a wedding. When the bridegroom spoke, it was poetry: "'She walks in beauty, like the night/Of cloudless climes and starry skies;'" he said, quoting Byron. "'And all that's best of dark and bright/Meet in her aspect and her eyes....'"

SERVES 6–8

4 egg whites

Pinch of salt

2 tablespoons sugar

4 egg yolks

2 tablespoons cornstarch

¼ teaspoon salt

½ cup sugar

2½ cups milk (preferably whole milk)

1 teaspoon vanilla extract

Nutmeg

Ground cinnamon

Cinnamon sticks (optional)

The bride's satin gown whispered across splintering floorboards as she passed, smiling, through the congregation and out into the early evening. The wedding dinner was a gift to her from the town for helping restore the church of San Rafael. In the gathering dusk in front of the church, the townspeople served a great Southwestern feast, which concluded with natillas in little paper cups.

Natillas (literally "creamies") is a fluffy liquid custard, simple to cook, serve, and sip. This traditional recipe comes from *Flora's Kitchen: Recipes from a New Mexico Family*, by Regina Romero. Appropriate for holidays and celebrations, "this delicious dessert was also served as a delightful breakfast," she notes, "or a soothing remedio for someone too sick to have a heavy meal."

IN A MEDIUM MIXING BOWL, beat the egg whites with the pinch of salt until soft peaks form, and then gradually add the 2 tablespoons of sugar. Set aside.

Thoroughly combine the egg yolks, cornstarch, ¼ teaspoon salt, and ½ cup sugar in a medium saucepan. Add the milk and cook over medium heat, stirring constantly, until the mixture has thickened nicely and coats the back of a spoon. (A clean finger drawn across the spoon will leave a clear line.) Do not let it boil.

Gently fold the vanilla and egg whites into the hot custard, which should cook them enough for safety. Serve immediately or chill before serving, but this dessert deflates quickly. Garnish with nutmeg, ground cinnamon, and optional cinnamon sticks.

Flan and Custard

MAKES 1 SINGLE 1-QUART FLAN
OR 6 INDIVIDUAL 6-OUNCE FLANS

Crème caramel certainly sounds more … well, *French* than the flat, sober Spanish word *flan*. But the two are almost identical. So is that other, even simpler product of chickens and cows known as baked custard, a homely Middle English cooking term that is unrelated, I trust, to "mustard" and "bustard," so I am giving the two recipes under one heading.

Flan always makes me think of Sor Juana Inés de la Cruz, a seventeenth-century nun who was one of Mexico's greatest poets and intellectuals. After working in her convent kitchen, she wrote a philosophical soliloquy on cooking and addressed it to her bishop. Eggs, she noted, behave quite differently depending on how they are separated, mixed, and heated. "Had Aristotle cooked, he would have written a great deal more," concluded Sor Juana subversively.

Children—and others—sometimes recoil from the slight bitterness of caramelized or "burnt" sugar, and they also may dislike the strong egg flavor and resilient texture created by the extra yolks that make a flan structurally sound enough to turn out of its mold. Milky baked custard is the gentle and nourishing pudding for them.

Flan
Caramel

¾ cup sugar

⅓ cup water

If your large mold is made of stovetop-safe metal, you can cook the caramel directly in it. If not, use a small saucepan. (To make the caramel spread more evenly on your porcelain or glass molds, warm them in a pan of hot water while you caramelize the sugar.) Place the sugar and water in the pan or mold, and swirl them over medium-high heat until the sugar dissolves.

Boil the syrup, swirling occasionally, for 3–5 minutes, or until it starts to change color. Watch carefully: it will turn from clear to yellow to gold to light brown. The desired color is a rich amber brown, but remember that the caramel will continue to cook briefly off the heat. When you think it is brown enough, remove it from the heat and, working fast, either tilt the mold to cover the bottom and sides with caramel, or pour the syrup into the warmed porcelain or glass molds and quickly tilt them to coat them with syrup. Set the mold or molds aside while you prepare the flan.

Flan

2½ cups milk (preferably whole milk)

3 eggs

3 egg yolks

½ cup sugar

1 teaspoon vanilla extract

Preheat the oven to 325 degrees F. In a small saucepan, warm the milk just until it starts to steam. Also bring a kettle of water to the simmer, which you will need later to bake the flan.

Meanwhile, beat the eggs and yolks together in a medium mixing bowl and gradually add the sugar, whisking until the mixture is light. Continue to beat as you slowly add the hot milk and vanilla. Strain the mixture into the prepared mold or molds set in a roasting or cake pan (space ramekins at least an inch apart). Pull out the lower oven rack, set the pan on it, and pour enough simmering water into the pan to reach halfway up the sides of the mold or ramekins.

Bake until the flan is barely set and a skewer inserted in the center comes out clean. Check every 15 minutes or so to make sure the water bath is not boiling, which will roughen the texture of the flan. If you see bubbles rising, add a bit of cool water. Baking time varies according to flan size and oven heat, ranging from 20–30 minutes for small shallow custard cups to more than an hour for large, deep flans.

Cool the flan in its mold on a wire rack. Flan is easiest to unmold when it has been well chilled. When you are ready to serve, run the tip of a knife around the edge of each flan, place a serving dish (deep enough to catch the caramel sauce) upside down over the mold, and quickly flip the two. Given a shake or two, the flan should drop neatly onto the dish. If it does not, dip the mold in warm water for a moment or two, and try again. Scrape out any remaining caramel, spoon it around the flan, and serve.

Baked Custard

SERVES 6

3 cups milk

3 eggs

½ cup sugar

¼ teaspoon salt

1 teaspoon vanilla extract

Nutmeg

Preheat the oven to 325 degrees F. Bring a kettle of water to the simmer. In a small saucepan, warm the milk just until it starts to steam. In a medium mixing bowl, beat the eggs until they are well blended. Add the sugar and salt. Then slowly add the hot milk, beating constantly, followed by the vanilla. Strain the custard into 1 large mold or 6 ramekins, sprinkle with nutmeg, and bake and test for doneness as for flan.

Spotted Pup

"*What* is the matter with Mary Jane?" inquires one of A. A. Milne's arch little poems for the very young. Meanwhile, in the Ernest Shepard illustration, a small girl furiously kicks off a shoe. "She's perfectly well and she hasn't a pain," the poem babbles on. *"And it's lovely rice pudding for dinner again!"*

Rice pudding really can be lovely. It's excellent for breakfast, and as arroz con leche it has long been enjoyed from one end of Latin America to the other. Probably that's how it came to the American West. Composed of simple, portable ingredients, and easy to make, it was a standby in cowboy camps, where a stingy cook might be called "so mean he'd bog [boil] a raisin and call it spotted pup." (Individual servings look especially puppy-like.)

But wait! Didn't the British Navy feed its sailors, after their weevily hardtack, "boiled baby" pudding, and buckets of grog, something called "spotted dog"? I notice in my great-grandparents' journals that rice was among the supplies they carried on their long, leisurely float trips down the Colorado at the turn of the last century. And that brings us back to little English Mary Jane.

Clearly rice pudding is ubiquitous, both in fluid, cream-soupy versions and in baked ones like this. Adapted from a dessert in *James Beard's American Cookery*, it's a good way to use leftover rice.

SERVES 6–8

½ cup raisins

¼ cup brandy, rum, or hot water

1–2 cups cooked rice (more if you prefer a solid pudding, less if not)

1 cup sugar, divided

1 teaspoon vanilla extract

5 eggs

2½ cups milk (preferably whole milk, or part half-and-half)

¼ teaspoon salt

Cinnamon or nutmeg (optional)

SOAK THE RAISINS in the brandy, rum, or hot water for 1 hour, or warm them briefly in the liquid over low heat or in a microwave oven. Preheat the oven to 350 degrees F.

In a medium mixing bowl, combine the rice, ½ cup of the sugar, the raisins and their soaking liquid, and the vanilla. In a large mixing bowl, beat the eggs and add the milk, salt, and remaining ½ cup of sugar. Stir in the rice mixture. If the rice was cooked without salt, you may wish to add more than ¼ teaspoon.

Pour the pudding into a buttered 2-quart casserole, or ladle it into 6–8 buttered ramekins, dividing the rice and raisins equally. Bake for 25–40 minutes, depending on the size of the mold, or until the surface is golden and lightly puffed. Either dust the pup with nutmeg or cinnamon, or leave it plain, and serve it either warm or cold. For the ultimate in spotted pups, add caramel sauce and cream.

Denver Pudding

SERVES 6–8

2 ounces chocolate, either unsweetened or semisweet

6 tablespoons butter

1 cup flour

1¼ cups sugar, divided

2 teaspoons baking powder

¼ teaspoon salt

½ cup milk

2 teaspoons vanilla extract

½ cup chopped nuts (optional)

½ cup packed brown sugar

4 tablespoons cocoa

1½ cups cold water or coffee

Why "Denver"? Perhaps it is because this recipe works well at high altitudes. Baking at altitude is a whole other world, as I know from baking mishaps in Denver, Mexico City, and our mountain ranch, where the house (and stove) sit at 4,500 feet. In such places it's helpful to have standbys like Denver Pudding that won't foam out of the pan and burn on the oven floor. This extremely lush, extremely easy pudding also masquerades under other names, such as "Hot Fudge Brownie Pudding," "Chocolate Brownie Pudding," and "Chocolate Pudding Cake." One of my favorite names is "Self-Saucing Pudding."

But Denver Pudding by any other name is just as great. If you bake it in a transparent container you will have the fun of watching a metamorphosis: it begins as a blob of batter topped with an alarming mess of loose ingredients, and it roils and boils and bakes into a nice island of chocolate cake afloat on a sea of hot fudge sauce. It's superb hot, warm, room-temperature, or chilled; and either plain or topped with whipped cream or ice cream.

Some commentators find Denver Pudding aesthetically lacking—unshapely—chaotic—even ugly!—and they suggest baking it for beauty's sake in individual dishes.

To them I say, "Pooh! Volcanoes are beautiful too."

PREHEAT THE OVEN to 350 degrees F. In a small saucepan, melt chocolate and butter together and set aside. In a large mixing bowl, whisk together the flour, ¾ cup sugar, baking powder, and salt. Blend in the milk and vanilla, followed by the chocolate mixture and the optional nuts. Pour the batter into a buttered 2-quart baking dish or an 8-inch-square pan, preferably of heatproof glass.

Now scatter across the top, without mixing, ½ cup sugar, ½ cup brown sugar, and 4 tablespoons cocoa. Pour the water or coffee over the top. Do not mix!

Bake for about 40 minutes, or until the volcanic island has formed above the sea. Serve either warm or cold.

Cherry Pudding

SERVES 6

1 cup sugar

1 cup flour

1 teaspoon baking soda

½ teaspoon salt

1 egg

1 15-ounce can cherries (packed in water)

⅓ cup packed brown sugar

1 tablespoon melted butter

½ cup chopped nuts

Close kin to cobbler, and also to cake, this cherry pudding takes very little effort, and it transforms pantry staples into a warm, fragrant fruit dessert. In 1953 we lived at a geological exploration camp in a remote corner of Utah, where my mother collected this recipe from our neighbor Sue Spencer. "I used to marvel at Sue, who lived in a small camp trailer with her husband, baby, and two little children," my mother says reminiscently. "She and her children were always perfectly groomed and dressed in clean clothes, hair ribbons, and so on." I myself clearly remember the deep red mud, the plague of gnats, the extraordinary reverberating blue of the sky, and the radioactive fallout from nuclear testing upwind of us. And even at the best of times, hair ribbons have always slithered right off my head.

"We shopped for groceries only once a month," my mother says, "and there was electricity only during the day. Water was hauled from a water trailer.... We all had a lot of fun."

It was during this epoch of our existence that the society editor of my parents' hometown newspaper called my grandmother and asked for an update on my mother's social life. What city was she living in now?

"Well, no city, actually. She's living in a canyon in Utah," my grandmother replied.

"What is she doing in a canyon?"

"Why, simply living there," said my grandmother.

Soon the society column announced: "Edith Lowell is living simply in a canyon."

PREHEAT THE OVEN to 325 degrees F. Whisk the sugar, flour, baking soda, and salt together in a large mixing bowl. Mix in the egg and the cherries, including their juice, and pour the batter into a buttered baking pan about 8 x 8 inches. Top with the brown sugar, butter, and nuts, and bake for about an hour, or until crisp on top. Serve warm or cold. Ice cream, whipped cream, or this cherry sauce make nice accompaniments.

Cherry Sauce

MAKES ABOUT 1½ CUPS

2 teaspoons cornstarch

½ cup water

1½ cups frozen sweet cherries or canned cherries, drained

¼ teaspoon almond extract

Pinch of ground cinnamon

In a small bowl, blend the cornstarch with 2 tablespoons of the water, then with the rest of the water. Place the cherries in a small saucepan, add the cornstarch and water mixture, and mix gently. Bring to a boil, stirring occasionally, and simmer just until the sauce thickens. Remove from the heat, add the almond extract and the cinnamon, and serve with cherry pudding.

Almendrado

SERVES 8–10

1 tablespoon unflavored gelatin

¼ cup cold water

1 cup boiling water

1 cup sugar

5 egg whites
(reserve the yolks for
the sauce; please see note
on eggs, page 9)

Pinch of salt

½ teaspoon almond extract

Red and green food coloring
(optional)

1 cup almonds, slivered or sliced

Where has all the almendrado gone? Forty years ago it was *the* fashionable dessert of Southwestern Mexican restaurants. It's airy, pretty, and, when tinted subtly red, green, and white to resemble the Mexican flag, patriotic to serve for either of the two Mexican independence days, Cinco de Mayo (May 5) and Diez y Seis de Septiembre (September 16). Almendrado, which means "almond-flavored," can also be made a day in advance for a Christmas party. This recipe comes from my cousin Peggy Cumming, who knows how to cook wonderful things by the side of the trail as well as at home in her ranch kitchen.

IN A MEDIUM MIXING BOWL, soak the gelatin in the cold water for about 5 minutes. Then add the boiling water and stir to dissolve the gelatin thoroughly. Add the sugar and stir again until it dissolves. Chill the mixture until it begins to stiffen; then beat it until it is frothy throughout.

In another medium bowl, beat the egg whites and salt until stiff peaks form, and fold them into the gelatin mixture. Add the almond extract, and beat until well blended. At this point, if you wish, divide the almendrado into three parts and tint one pink and one pale green. Line a large (9 x 5-inch, or 2-quart) loaf pan with wax paper, allowing the strips to extend above the rim of the pan. Layer the almendrado to resemble *la Bandera:* first green, then white, then pink. Cover it lightly, and refrigerate it until it sets. Meanwhile, make the sauce.

Almond Custard Sauce

MAKES ABOUT 3 CUPS

2 cups milk

5 egg yolks

¼ cup sugar

⅛ teaspoon salt

1 teaspoon vanilla extract

1 cup cream

Scald the milk in a double boiler over hot, but not boiling, water. In a medium mixing bowl, beat the egg yolks lightly, add the sugar and salt, beat well, and gradually pour the hot milk into this mixture. Return the custard to the top of the double boiler, and cook it, stirring constantly, until the mixture thickens and coats the back of a spoon. Do not let it boil. When it cools, add the vanilla and the cream, whipped stiff in another bowl.

Serve almendrado sliced, garnished with sauce, and sprinkled with toasted almonds. *¡Viva México!*

Clouds in the Sky

SERVES 6–8

2 teaspoons soft butter

¼ cup powdered sugar

12 egg whites (about 1⅔ cups), at room temperature

½ teaspoon cream of tartar

⅛ teaspoon salt

1½ cups sugar (preferably superfine or baker's sugar)

1 teaspoon vanilla extract

To serve clouds for dessert, set a pouf of meringue adrift in a sky of sauce.

The inspiration for this recipe is old-fashioned Floating Island, known as *oeufs à la neige*, or "snowy eggs" in French. But that dish includes yellow custard sauce, which would look more like tornado weather than a serene Western atmosphere. So here are two light, fruit-flavored liquid skies: blueberry for high noon and raspberry for sunset.

Soft Baked Meringue

Preheat the oven to 250 degrees F. Use the soft butter to coat the inside of a 4-quart baking dish, approximately 9 x 13 inches and 3 inches deep, and preferably ceramic or glass, though metal will do. Sift or sieve the powdered sugar evenly over the buttered surface, and knock out the excess.

Using an electric mixer and a large mixing bowl, beat the egg whites at medium speed until they are frothy. Then add the cream of tartar and salt, and continue to beat, gradually increasing the speed, until soft peaks form.

Slowly add the sugar by tablespoonfuls or by pouring it in a very thin stream, and beat the meringue for 4–5 minutes, or until it forms stiff, shiny peaks. Beat in the vanilla. Then scrape the meringue into the prepared dish, leaving the top somewhat irregular.

Set it at the lower middle level of the oven, and bake for 30–40 minutes, or until a cake tester inserted in the middle comes out clean. The meringue will rise at least 3 inches as it bakes, but it will sink down to its original height as it cools on a wire rack. When it is cool, either serve it with sauce, or cover it and keep it refrigerated for several days. Wrapped airtight, it can be frozen for several weeks.

To serve, cut the meringue in irregular, cloud-shaped servings and arrange each one upon a bed of sauce. Garnish, if desired, with paper parasols, Caramel or Chocolate Lightning (see page 49), or fresh berries.

Blue Sky Sauce

MAKES ABOUT 1½ CUPS

12 ounces (2–3 cups) blueberries, frozen or fresh

¼ cup water

⅓ cup sugar (or more, to taste)

⅛ teaspoon ground cinnamon

⅛ teaspoon salt

2–3 teaspoons lemon juice (to taste)

¼–½ teaspoon grated lemon zest (optional)

1–2 tablespoons raspberry liqueur (optional)

Blue food coloring (optional)

Wash and pick over fresh blueberries. Place the berries, water, ⅓ cup sugar, cinnamon, and salt in a medium saucepan over medium heat, and bring to a simmer, stirring. Cook just until the sugar dissolves and the berries are hot (1–2 minutes).

Puree the mixture until it is smooth in a food processor or blender, and strain it through a fine sieve into a small bowl, pressing on the residue to extract all the puree. Add the lemon juice, and taste. Then add more sugar, lemon juice, and the optional lemon zest and raspberry liqueur if desired or necessary for flavor. Chill before serving, and add a little additional water if the sauce has thickened. (You may wish to enhance the blue color with a drop or two of blue food coloring.)

NOTE Unless you have perfect berries at the peak of the season, good frozen berries may be more flavorful in these recipes than fresh ones, which can be saved for garnish.

VARIATION I: SUNSET SAUCE Substitute raspberries or strawberries (or a combination of the two) for the blueberries, hulling and slicing the strawberries if they are fresh. Omit the cinnamon.

VARIATION II: CREAMY SKY SAUCE Whip 1 cup of heavy cream. Fold it gently into the cold blue or red berry sauce just before serving. This is very good.

WHAT'S YOUR PREFERENCE? A humble fruit cobbler baked outdoors in a Dutch oven, or a French tart served with panache in a trendy restaurant? You could find either pie almost anywhere in the American West today. Or you could stay home and make one easily yourself. Bits of my mother's leftover pie crust, sprinkled with cinnamon sugar and probably rather gray from much manipulation, were the first "pies" I ever baked.

Pie may boast the widest range of any member of the dessert family, since it pops up in so many food niches: from utterly homespun to haute cuisine, from sweet to savory, and from hot to ice-cold. Here are a few excellent pies, tarts, and turnovers. The cinnamon-sugar crust bits don't really require a recipe, just a small child to make and eat them.

Classic Pie Crust

Many otherwise fearless cooks are afraid of pie crust. I never felt sure about the stuff either, until I had a lesson from Mildred Probst, a dear friend and neighbor and a marvelous baker. The experience of watching her work with flour and dough absolutely illuminated for me the meaning of the phrase "a light hand with pastry." She pushed a little pile of flour off to the side and added it to her dough with flicks of her fingertips—never too much at a time. I think of her with gratitude every time I make a pie, partly because I take out my notes from the day she taught me. I recorded the recipe on the back of a sheet of pizza discount coupons from 1984 or 1985, judging by the scribbles added by my daughter Anna, who was still writing all in capitals at the time, and signing her name with two backward Ns.

Mrs. Probst was a dove-shaped lady with a dove-like chuckle. But as a Midwestern farm girl and the wife of a Presbyterian minister, she knew how to make, do, and cope with almost anything, including a parishioner who accidentally—but repeatedly!—cut off his fingers in an electric fan. She, like my grandfather, was one of the last of the covered-wagon children, sturdy travelers who lived to cross the same ground in jets. But a good pie is still a good pie. Actually, pies were only a sideline for Mrs. Probst; her greatest masterpieces, perhaps, were feather-light dinner rolls and delectable Christmas stollen.

When she baked, she sifted her flour straight into her measuring cups with a small sifter that she kept in the flour bin, so that is how these measurements should be made. For pie crust she favored a method of working the shortening into the flour in two batches, which gives the cook more control over the texture. I used to be afraid to over-wet and overwork my dough, but she advised me to add more water, and my crusts have stayed together better ever since. For rolling out her pastry Mrs. Probst used a rolling-pin cover and pastry cloth, both lightly floured. I find this helps to control sticking and tearing, and although I still do a fair amount of patchwork, I just don't worry about it. I know the crust will be good anyway, as long as I touch it lightly.

MAKES 2 PIE CRUSTS (9-INCH)

2¼ cups sifted flour

1 teaspoon salt

⅞ cup shortening (¾ cup plus 2 tablespoons; may be part butter or lard)

5 tablespoons ice water

PREPARE THE ICE WATER. Whisk the flour and salt together in a large mixing bowl. Add ⅝ cup (½ cup plus 2 tablespoons) shortening, and work it thoroughly into the flour and salt with your fingers until the texture is as fine as cornmeal. For easier blending, if you wish to use part butter or lard—which makes excellent pastry—add it all at once, either with the first or second batch of shortening.

Now mix the remaining ¼ cup shortening into the dough, first by cutting it in with a table knife, and then by working with your fingers. Stop sooner than before, when the lumps are pea-sized. Add the ice water tablespoon by tablespoon, tossing the dough with the fork until it clings together. Be sure to add all of the water and possibly more. If the dough seems sticky, let it rest for a minute or two, and, if necessary, flour it very lightly before you gather it into a ball and remove it from the bowl.

Divide it into two equal portions, form them gently into disks about 1 inch thick, wrap them airtight, and refrigerate them for at least an hour, or as long as 2 days. This allows the gluten in the dough to relax. Pie crust disks can also be stored in a freezer for a month or so. Thaw before using.

To roll out a crust, dust with flour the pastry cloth, rolling-pin cover, and disk of dough. If the dough is stiff and cold, allow it to warm briefly. For an even thickness, try not to run the pin over the edge of the dough. To transfer the raw crust to a pie pan, either fold the dough carefully in quarters, match the point of the folded dough to the center of the pan, and unfold; or roll the dough up on your pin, and then unroll it over the pan.

Either way, it is important to trim (and patch) the overlapping crust to an even width around the edge of the pan, or else it will distort as it bakes. Set out a small bowl of water while you're shaping your crust. Patches will not adhere successfully unless they are attached with water—a wet fingertip works nicely. Now flute the rim of the crust, or mark it decoratively with a fork, wrap the pie shell, and refrigerate it for 30 minutes or so before baking.

Apple Empanadas

Empanadas—or "embreaded ones"—are probably the commonest pies in Spanish-speaking regions. A circle of dough encloses either a meat or a sweet filling, most commonly mashed pumpkin or squash. Occasionally empanadas contain brown sugar or custard, but the tastiest filling of all is probably apple. Empanadas freeze very well and pack up nicely in picnics and lunches.

MAKES 12 TO 15 EMPANADAS,
ABOUT 5 INCHES IN DIAMETER

1 recipe Classic Pie
Crust (page 94)

4 medium apples such as Granny
Smiths or Golden Delicious

1–2 teaspoons lemon juice

¼ teaspoon ground cinnamon

½ teaspoon vanilla extract

2–4 tablespoons sugar

MAKE AND REFRIGERATE the crust. Peel and core the apples, and chop them into ½-inch chunks. Sprinkle with lemon juice, cinnamon, vanilla, and 2 tablespoons sugar. Taste and add more sugar if necessary.

Either divide the dough into 12–15 balls and roll each one into a separate small round, or roll all the crust at once. Then, using a small tart pan or a plastic lid as a guide, cut circles 5–6 inches in diameter. Either way, transfer them to a baking sheet lined with parchment paper. Spoon 2–3 tablespoons of chopped apples in the middle of the lower half of each circle, staying about 1 inch from the edge. Don't overfill. Moisten the rim of the dough with water, fold each empanada in half, and then seal the edge with a series of small pleats. Repeat with the rest of the dough and apples. To help them hold their shape, refrigerate empanadas for an hour or freeze them for 30 minutes before baking. (Frozen, they will keep perfectly for up to 3 months and can be baked directly from the freezer.)

To bake, preheat the oven to 400 degrees F. Brush the tops of the empanadas with milk or water and sprinkle with sugar, if you like. Bake them for 20–30 minutes, depending on their starting temperature, or until they are golden brown on top and toasty brown on the bottom. Serve warm or at room temperature.

Peach Cobbler

SERVES 6

½ cup butter or margarine

I cup flour

I cup sugar

I teaspoon baking powder

½ teaspoon salt

I cup milk

I egg

3–4 cups good-quality peaches, fresh, frozen, or canned (drained)

The original Early American cobbler was, besides a shoemaker, an alcoholic drink with ice and fruit bobbing around in it. How fruit punch transformed itself into a hot baked dessert is a real mystery … unless thrifty cooks baked the left-over fruit under some sort of crust the following day.

How does a cobbler differ from a crisp, a crumble, a crunch, a slump, a grunt, or a brown Betty? The answer is, "Not much." They are all examples of country cooking, not even requiring a bake oven. And all of them are American relatives of the Italian crostata and the French clafouti.

"There seems to be a lot of cobbler around here," murmured a newcomer to Lubbock, Texas, when asked recently about local specialties. And cobbler did apparently flourish all along the Western frontier, becoming a favorite ranch and chuck wagon dish, as it bakes very well in a Dutch oven. (Dutch oven cookery, like barbecuing, is often but not exclusively a male art.) This version of cobbler is a compilation of dozens I have found, including one called "Dude Food," and several by Stella Hughes, the author of *Chuck Wagon Cookin'*, where she also gives recipes for Bear Fat Pie Crust, Tallow Pudding, Poorman's Cake, Damned Hot Chili, and S.O.B. Stew.

PREHEAT THE OVEN to 350 degrees F. Melt the butter in the oven in a 2–3 quart baking dish. Dish size is somewhat flexible, but bear in mind that the shallower the cobbler, the quicker it will bake. When the butter is melted, remove the pan from the oven.

Meanwhile, mix the flour, sugar, baking powder, and salt in a medium bowl. Blend in the milk and the egg and beat the batter until it is smooth. Pour the batter into the prepared pan, and scatter the peaches over the top. Bake until the top is nicely browned, 30–45 minutes. Serve warm or at room temperature, with or without cream or ice cream.

The recipe doubles easily and travels well.

VARIATION I: OTHER FRUIT Try the recipe with nectarines, apricots, cherries, apples, pears, or berries, or a carefully selected combination.

VARIATION II: CAST-IRON OLD-TIME DUTCH OVEN COBBLER This recipe requires an old-fashioned cast-iron Dutch oven with feet and a heavy iron lid flat enough to hold hot coals.

While your good, big hardwood fire burns down to red coals (this will take about an hour), prepare the cobbler, first melting the butter in a Dutch oven set over the fire. Get the oven quite hot, but don't burn the butter. Also preheat the lid until it is evenly hot, but not red-hot.

Pour the fruit and batter into the oven. Place the filled oven on a level bed of coals, bank more coals around the edges of the oven, and pile still more around the rim of the lid. To check on the baking, peek by lifting the lid carefully with your iron "gonch hook" (from the Spanish *gancho,* or hook). But be very careful not to spill ashes on your cobbler, and remember that every time you open the lid, you lose heat. You can also tell a lot about the state of your cobbler by using your nose. Is it baking? Or is it burning?

To insure even heat, occasionally use the hook to give the oven a quarter turn. If the cobbler cooks too fast on the bottom, move it off the bed of coals. If it bakes too fast on the top, remove the coals from the lid. Take the cobbler off the fire a little before you think it's done because it will continue to bake in the hot oven while it waits to be served.

Chocolate Pecan Pie

MAKES 1 PIE (9-INCH)

2 ounces unsweetened chocolate

3 tablespoons butter

1 cup light corn syrup

¾ cup sugar

3 eggs

½ teaspoon salt

1 teaspoon vanilla extract

1½ cups chopped pecans

9-inch unbaked pie shell (½ recipe Classic Pie Crust, page 94)

1 cup pecan halves

In this superb creation, bitter chocolate beautifully counterbalances the often extreme sweetness of pecan pie. Beneath the crisp nut topping, the filling resembles a chocolate pudding, lush but not cloyingly sweet. Highly recommended by Nan Stockholm Walden, whose roasted pecans appear under Small Confections, this pie has been chosen as the featured recipe on the Green Valley Pecan Company brochure.

PREHEAT THE OVEN to 375 degrees F. Melt the chocolate and butter together in a small saucepan over very low heat, or in a microwave, stirring several times. In another small saucepan, simmer the corn syrup and the sugar together for 2 minutes, or until the sugar dissolves. Add the chocolate mixture to the syrup mixture, stir, and allow this blend to cool somewhat.

Then, in a large mixing bowl, beat the eggs with the salt, and gradually add the chocolate syrup, beating constantly. Blend in the vanilla and chopped pecans, and pour the filling into the unbaked pie shell. Arrange a neat design of pecan halves on top. Bake at the middle level of the preheated oven for 35–40 minutes, or until the filling is lightly set. (It will not be firm.) Cool before serving.

This pie needs no garnish.

Frozen Prickly Pear Chiffon Pie

MAKES 1 PIE (9-INCH)

8½ double graham crackers

½ cup pecan
halves, slightly toasted

½ teaspoon ground cinnamon

3 tablespoons sugar

⅓ cup butter, melted

Airy, cool, and delicate, a frozen fruit chiffon pie comes as the perfect finish to a meal including chile or any other food with lots of vim and zing. This convenient recipe may be made days or weeks ahead and kept frozen. It is best decorated just before serving, and it tastes loveliest when partially thawed.

Nut Crumb Crust

Break the crackers roughly into a food processor. Add the pecans, cinnamon, and sugar, and process them until the mixture resembles fine crumbs. Add the melted butter and pulse until just combined. If the mixture seems too dry to hold its shape, add another tablespoon of melted butter.

If you do not have a processor, seal the crackers in a heavy plastic bag and crush them with a rolling pin, or use a blender. Grind the nuts in a blender or other device. Mix all of the ingredients in a medium bowl, dribble in the butter, and stir well.

1 teaspoon grated lemon zest

2 egg yolks

2 tablespoons sugar

3 tablespoons lemon juice

⅛ teaspoon salt

2 tablespoons soft butter

⅓ cup prickly pear syrup

⅔ cup cream

2 egg whites, at room
temperature (please see note on
eggs, page 9)

¼ teaspoon cream of tartar

2 tablespoons sugar

Additional whipped cream
(optional)

Raspberries or sliced
strawberries or prickly pear
fruit (optional)

Additional prickly
pear syrup (optional)

Then press the crust mixture into the pie pan, using a piece of plastic wrap for neatness if necessary. Use a flat-bottomed glass to tamp the crust evenly into the bottom and up the sides of the pan. Lightly pat the rim smooth. Then chill the crust, covered, until you are ready to fill it.

NOTE Before cutting the pie, release the crust from the pan by wrapping the bottom of the pan briefly in a hot, wet kitchen towel. Or carefully submerge the bottom of the pie dish in a shallow pan of hot water for a few seconds (a skillet works perfectly). This will melt the butter in the crust just enough to permit you to cut neat slices.

PLACE THE LEMON ZEST in a medium mixing bowl. In a small saucepan, whisk together the egg yolks and 2 tablespoons sugar until they are light and fluffy. Add the lemon juice, salt, and butter, and cook the mixture over low to medium heat, stirring, until it thickens, becomes opaque, and coats the back of a spoon. It will curdle if it boils, so watch carefully. When a clean finger leaves a clear trail across the back of a spoon, pour the mixture through a fine strainer into the bowl with the lemon zest, add the prickly pear syrup, and blend thoroughly. Cool it to lukewarm.

Meanwhile, chill a medium mixing bowl and whip the cream in it. Delicately blend the cooled prickly pear mixture into the cream, cover, and refrigerate. In a medium mixing bowl, whip the egg whites until they are foamy, add the cream of tartar, and beat until they hold soft peaks. Then add the remaining sugar, 1 tablespoon at a time, and beat until the mixture holds stiff peaks. Delicately fold it into the chilled prickly pear cream, and turn the cream into the pie shell, smoothing the top. Freeze uncovered until firm, and then wrap airtight. Decorate with whipped cream, fruit, or prickly pear syrup before serving, if desired.

VARIATION: FROZEN LIME CHIFFON PIE Substitute 2 teaspoons grated lime zest for the lemon zest, and lime juice for the lemon juice. Simmer the lime zest with the sugar, yolks, lime juice, salt, and butter, and strain it out of the custard before proceeding, since lime zest is too bitter to leave in the pie. Omit the prickly pear syrup, and add a drop or two of green food coloring if you want the pie to appear green (lime juice is naturally pale yellow, not green). Before serving, decorate the pie with whipped cream and additional grated lime zest, if desired.

Chocolate Mousse Tarts

**MAKES 24–30 TARTS
(2½-INCH) OR A 10-INCH PIE**

2 (9-ounce) packages Nabisco "Famous Chocolate Wafers"

7–8 ounces (⅞–1 cup) unsalted butter, melted

16 ounces bittersweet chocolate (such as Lindt's Excellence, Valrhona's Extra Bitter, or Baker's Bittersweet)

2 eggs (please see note on eggs, page 9)

4 egg yolks

1 quart cream, divided

⅔ cup powdered sugar, divided

4 egg whites

Chocolate curls or grated chocolate for garnish, optional (directions follow)

Donna Nordin's fabulous chocolate mousse pie appears on the menu of Café Terra Cotta in Tucson, Arizona. Adapted from her recipe, these tarts provide much the same chocolate bliss, but on a smaller scale for lighter appetites. They freeze beautifully for several months, wrapped airtight and ready to receive their final decoration before serving.

LINE 24 CUPCAKE TINS with paper-lined foil cupcake liners, or set out 24–30 individual 2½-inch tart pans with removable bottoms, and grease them with vegetable oil or cooking spray. (Shallow tart pans will produce more tarts.) Pulverize the cookies in a food processor or blender, add the melted butter, and pulse or blend until well mixed. If the crust seems too dry, add a little more melted butter. Then press equal portions of warm crust mixture into the bottoms and up the sides of the cupcake liners or the tart pans. Refrigerate the tart shells until they are firm.

In a double boiler over hot but not boiling water (or over very low heat, or in a microwave), melt the chocolate, stirring until smooth. Remove it from the heat and beat in the whole eggs and the egg yolks. In a chilled medium bowl, whip 2 cups of cream with ⅓ cup powdered sugar. Fold the whipped cream into the chocolate mixture. Then whip the egg whites until stiff peaks form, and fold them into the chocolate mixture. Spoon the filling into the chilled tart shells, cover, and refrigerate overnight or until firm; or freeze for up to 3 months, wrapped airtight.

To serve, whip the remaining cream with the remaining sugar. If you wish, remove each tart from its paper liner and replace in the foil liner for serving, or serve tarts unmolded from their pans. You may simply top each tart with cream, or you may put the cream in a pastry bag fitted with a large star tip, and pipe decorative cream around the tops (and bottoms, if you like) of the tarts. Decorate with optional chocolate curls or grated chocolate. Boxed or wrapped very carefully, the decorated tarts may be frozen for several weeks. Thaw just before serving.

CHOCOLATE CURLS With a vegetable peeler, scrape the curls from a bar of bittersweet chocolate at room temperature.

GRATED CHOCOLATE To make a mixture of coarse and fine flakes, grate a room-temperature bar of bittersweet chocolate on various sides of a box grater.

VARIATION: CHOCOLATE MOUSSE PIE (*Serves 12–16*) Instead of using the tart pans or cupcake liners, grease the sides of a 10-inch springform pan with vegetable oil or cooking spray. Press the warm crust mixture evenly onto the bottom and sides of the pan, and refrigerate it while you prepare the filling. Fill the pie, and chill it overnight before decorating it: first, spread a layer of whipped cream on top; then remove the pie from the pan, and finish by piping cream around the top rim and sprinkling the pie with chocolate curls or grated chocolate, or both. Frozen and then boxed, a very carefully wrapped pie may be kept in the freezer for several weeks. Thaw just before serving.

Frozen Desserts

IN THE DAYS BEFORE CARS WERE AIR-CONDITIONED, our trips across the desert in summer used to begin before dawn. We stopped sometimes for a while at the height of the heat, as we did one day in the farming town of Coolidge, Arizona, when I was two and my brother was a baby. Probably the temperature was 110 degrees, maybe higher, for Coolidge lies in a low, flat place where heat accumulates. We parked in the roasting shade at a little frozen custard stand, perhaps a Dairy Queen, and everyone, including the baby, ate ice cream. I remember it well: cold, cold, sweet vanilla cream, melting, melting, melting, yet still cool. Ah!

I also remember a perplexity that bothered me for many years afterward. If that place was so terribly hot, why did they ever name it "Coolidge"?

Actually, a less-creamy delicacy like lemon ice probably tastes even better than ice cream on a scorching day, so this selection of favorite frozen desserts runs from very simple ice pops to the Grand Canyon Ice Cream Cake, which is appropriate for winter as well as summertime.

Prickly Pear Lemonade Pops

For a brief period of my childhood, we lived in an actual neighborhood with sidewalks, next-door playmates, and an ice cream truck. Even Kokopelli would be practically powerless next to an ice cream man playing his weird little tune in a neighborhood full of children on a long, hot summer day. Back then I liked "Bullets" best, and those layered, violently colored cylinders of ice were the inspiration for these homemade frozen sunsets, quick to make and quick to melt away from your freezer.

MAKES 4 POPS (5 OUNCES EACH)

About 1¼ cups lemonade (either the recipe on page 78 or a good one made from concentrate)

1–2 tablespoons prickly pear syrup (or raspberry, boysenberry, or other red fruit syrup)

FILL ICE-POP MOLDS or small paper cups halfway with lemonade, using about ⅔ cup. Freeze until the lemonade is almost solid but still soft enough to insert a stick, handle, or plastic spoon. Then add syrup to the remaining lemonade until it reaches the shade of pink and the taste you like. Pour the prickly pear lemonade into the molds, add handles, and freeze solid. The goal is to cause some of the pink lemonade to filter down into the yellow lemonade, creating interesting sunset effects.

VARIATIONS Instead of lemonade, you can use orange, white grape, pineapple, or white cranberry juice. Instead of juice colored with prickly pear or other syrup, you can substitute red juices such as cranberry, cranberry-raspberry, cherry, or grape. (After Mount Pinatubo erupted in the Philippines in 1991, sunsets across the American Southwest immediately turned a deep fruity purple.)

Raspado de Frutas

SERVES 1

Fruit sorbet, softened, any flavor

Chopped fruit, either fresh, canned, or frozen, to match or harmonize with the sorbet

Vanilla ice cream, softened

Many times when I take St. Mary's Road west across the Santa Cruz River, which cuts through the heart of Tucson, Arizona, I think of my Uncle Gilbert. When he was a small boy, around 1908, he used to wade the river every morning to reach Davis School, which still stands on the east side. Now there is a bridge, and the river is dry. Back then, on days when Uncle Gilbert didn't feel particularly academic, he would lie down in the Santa Cruz until he was so wet and muddy that the teachers would send him home from school to change.

Today as a boy came out of the river—if there were a river—he'd see a sign that reads "OASIS FRUIT CONES," and below that, in smaller letters, "RASPADOS DE FRUTAS." Below that, a painted penguin stands on an ice floe beneath a palm tree, contemplating many huge fruits that lie at his feet like red, orange, and yellow soccer balls. In his wing he holds a white cone, but in fact if you join the line that usually forms there in hot weather, your *raspado* will come in a large paper cup. It will consist of two parts: an outer layer of shaved ice or slush mixed with chunks of fruit, and an inner filling of vanilla ice cream. You will be glad you stopped. It's almost as good as a roll in the river.

This recipe doesn't even try to duplicate a true Oasis Fruit Cone. It merely glances appreciatively in that direction. It doesn't want to get into the problem of crushing or shaving ice in its home kitchen. Sometimes it is lazy. Besides, it likes sorbet.

IN A SMALL MIXING BOWL, blend about ¼ cup chopped fruit with the softened sorbet. Spread the mixture on the bottom and up the sides of an ice cream cone, parfait glass, or other serving cup. Fill the center with ice cream, add a spoon, and serve.

Pre-packed into small paper cups, each with a plastic spoon frozen in place, this makes a nice summer dessert for children. It should always be eaten outdoors, if possible.

Rocky Mountain Sundae

SERVES 1 OR MORE

Rocky road ice cream

Chocolate sauce
(see page 116)

Whipped cream

Chocolate-covered almonds or
other small chocolate candies

Slivered almonds, toasted

Salted nuts, such as peanuts,
pecans, or cashews

Miniature marshmallows

Depending on the size you make your peaks, you may need several mountaineers to do justice to one of these sundaes.

FORM "MOUNTAINS" by molding softened ice cream in various sizes of paper cups, from tiny to medium. Refreeze until serving time. Then either cut away the paper cups or warm them briefly with a hot, wet towel or a dip in warm water, and unmold them on a serving plate. Add a chocolate lava flow, top the peaks with whipped cream snow, and scatter other rock formations upon and around the mountains. Serve immediately.

Saguaro Sundae

The giant saguaro cactus, or *Carnegiea gigantea*, is very important in its native Sonoran Desert for biological, practical, and symbolic reasons. Its fruit plays a crucial role in sustaining the desert ecosystem—including the human members of that system. Every May and June a few devotees, mainly members of the Tohono O'odham Nation, still painstakingly harvest the streaky red fruits and either eat them fresh, freeze them, or process them into a garnet-colored syrup, which can then be further transformed into a sacramental cactus wine, or into a truly extraordinary ice cream sundae. (Prickly pear syrup hints at the flavor, as does an excellent raspberry coulis, or a fine Pinot Noir.)

A fuller account of the saguaro, including harvesting information, may be found in *Saguaro: The Desert Giant*, which I wrote with my daughter Anna Humphreys, and where these recipes first appeared, in a slightly different form.

Traditional Saguaro Syrup

Ripe saguaro fruit, both fresh and sun-dried

Water

Get up as early as possible. Harvest the fruit with a picking pole (called *kuipaD* in O'odham) and waterproof basket. Balance your basket on your head, and carry it back to camp. Remove all inedible material from the fruit, and reserve any sun-dried fruit to cook later. Break off the dark, hardened calyx of the saguaro flower, and use it as a tool to split the fresh fruit and scoop out the pulp, or use your fingernails.

Collect the pulp in a large clay cooking pot (*hi-to-ta-kut*), cover with at least an equal amount of water, knead it thoroughly, and allow it to soak until the liquid is deep red (sometimes as long as a day, but the sooner the better, as it spoils quickly).

Boil this deep-red mixture over a lively wood fire, stirring frequently with a wooden ladle to extract the sugar and flavor. When the pulp is cooked and rises to the top, strain the contents of the pot through a special basket made of sotol (desert spoon) leaves, removing cactus fiber and seeds and reserving all liquid. Spread the pulpy material on a mat in the sun to dry. Wash all sand and sediment from the cooking pot, return the liquid to it, and boil it again, skimming off the foam, until its darkened, reddish-brown color and slightly thickened texture show that it has reached the desired concentration.

Hermetically seal the syrup in clean, narrow-necked clay jars (*si-to-ta-kut*), covering the tops with potsherds cemented to the jars with mud. This way the syrup, if not used for wine or other purposes, will keep as long as a year.

Cook the sun-dried fruit later in a separate batch (once dry, it will not spoil).

Modern Saguaro Syrup

Ripe saguaro fruit, both fresh and sun-dried

Water

Get up as early as possible. Harvest the fruit with a picking pole and plastic buckets. Back at camp, remove all inedible materials from the fruit and reserve any sun-dried fruit in a plastic bag to cook later.

Scoop out the pulp from ripe fruit with a small knife, or your fingernails, and collect it in a bucket. Cover it with water, knead thoroughly, and allow it to soak until the liquid is deep red, at least 30 minutes and maybe longer (under refrigeration this time can be extended safely to a day).

Transfer the soaked fruit and liquid to a 4-gallon enamelware cooking pot and boil, stirring frequently, over a lively wood fire (or medium heat on a stove) for about 30 minutes, stirring to extract the sugar and flavor. When the pulp is cooked and rises to the top, strain the mixture first through window-screen mesh to remove all pulp and seeds, and then through a flour sack to remove fine sediment. Reserve all liquid. Spread the pulpy material on window screens in the sun to dry. Return the liquid to a clean pot and boil, skimming any foam, for at least 30 minutes and up to several hours, until a darkened, reddish-brown color and slightly thickened texture show that it has reached the desired concentration. Seal the syrup in clean recycled glass jars of various sizes, such as pickle jars or baby food jars. Refrigerate for long-term storage.

Cook the sun-dried fruit later in a separate batch (once dry, it will not spoil).

SERVES 1

Saguaro Sundae

Saguaro syrup (see previous recipes)

Vanilla ice cream

Spoon 2–3 tablespoons of syrup over each serving of ice cream.

Lemon Ice

You can make great lemon ice with simple kitchen tools, or you can use the very latest imported gelato freezer. The taste will be equally good. (Actually, though, this ice is closer to a granita than it is to a gelato.) By lowering the freezing point, a small amount of alcohol promotes finer crystals and a smoother texture, but it is not necessary. My daughter Mary has also substituted the Italian homemade liqueur called *limoncello* for the vodka, with great success.

If you live in citrus country, here's a fine solution to the problem that our friend Kyleen calls "Ton-O-Lemons."

SERVES 6

1 cup fresh lemon juice
(or fresh-squeezed and frozen)

⅛ teaspoon salt

1 cup sugar (if possible, baker's
or superfine)

2¼ cups water (use bottled, if
your tap water is not delicious)

2 tablespoons vodka (optional for
smoother texture)

IN A 3-QUART stainless-steel or ceramic mixing bowl, combine all these ingredients. Whisk until the sugar dissolves, place the covered bowl in the refrigerator to chill thoroughly, and then follow the manufacturer's directions for your ice cream freezer.

Alternatively, place the bowl directly in the freezing compartment of your refrigerator for about 1 hour, or until ice begins to form on the top and sides. Now beat the mixture thoroughly with a wire whisk, and return it to the freezer, whisking approximately every 30 minutes for 3–5 hours, or until it reaches a slushy consistency. If the ice freezes too hard, simply let it warm briefly and beat again. Serve it promptly in chilled dishes. If it melts, drink it.

VARIATION: MARGARITA ICE Substitute fresh-squeezed lime juice for half of the lemon juice, and in place of vodka, use a good tequila.

Grand Canyon Ice Cream Cake

The Grand Canyon is one of many great canyons, perhaps the most magnificent. But Canyon de Chelly is exquisite, Bryce and Zion are baroque, the Barranca del Cobre is enormous and exotic, and to me little Thomas Canyon, hidden away in Southern Arizona with Baboquivari Peak rising above it, is the most beautiful of all.

As a geologist's daughter I have enjoyed trying to match some of the ancient layers of rock with flavors of cake and ice cream. My father's geological models, which I remember well from his graduate-student days, also featured fascinating but inedible layers of plaster of paris and aluminum powder.

It took time to make the Grand Canyon, and it takes time to make this dessert, but fortunately nothing like 1.7 billion years. Each of the various elements is simple in itself, most can be bought ready-made, and all can be assembled separately and stored or frozen until the right geological moment arrives. Then you re-create the Western Wonder of the World in your kitchen.

My grandfather, who worked at the Grand Canyon as a young engineer in the 1920s, used to swim across the Colorado before the dams upstream blocked the rich reddish-brown sediment that gave the river its name. He told me that to him the Colorado looked and felt like "chocolate soup." So the finishing touch here is a chocolate sauce in honor of him and the free Colorado.

For each Grand Canyon dessert you will need
- 1 cake layer, 9 inches by at least 1½ inches thick (either the Orange-Almond Cake on page 53, or the One-Egg Cake on page 37, or your choice)
- At least 3, and preferably more, contrasting colors and flavors of ice cream, sherbet, or sorbet, such as chocolate, vanilla, orange, raspberry, boysenberry, coffee, strawberry, and chocolate chip—you will need 2–3 quarts in all
- Chocolate meringue buttes and boulders (recipe follows)
- Chocolate sauce (recipes follow)
- Optional garnishes: Cocoa, chocolate sprinkles, nuts, and assorted candy rocks and pebbles, such as chocolate-covered almonds, broken chocolate bars, "rock" candy, etc.

This suggested cake has a chocolate-fruit-nut theme, but you can of course interpret the recipe with any of your favorite flavors and textures and create your own canyon. Here's a layout that distantly approximates the Grand Canyon. Properly speaking, the lower third of the cake should be made of chocolate, and then the cook should drop the whole thing heavily on the kitchen floor, pick up the pieces, and start again on top of the ruins, reproducing a phenomenon that geologists poetically call the Great Unconformity.

- Chocolate Meringue Buttes and Boulders (surface rock formations)
- Orange-Almond Cake (Kaibab Limestone)
- Chocolate chip ice cream (Toroweap Formation)
- Orange sorbet (Coconino Sandstone)
- Raspberry sorbet (Redwall Limestone)
- Chocolate ice cream (Vishnu Schist)
- Chocolate River Sauce (Colorado River)

Chocolate Meringue Buttes and Boulders

2 tablespoons cocoa

1 cup powdered sugar

4 large egg whites, room temperature

½ teaspoon cream of tartar

½ cup sugar, preferably baker's or superfine sugar

3–4 drops red food coloring (liquid, not paste)

Line two baking sheets with parchment paper, or grease and flour them thoroughly. Preheat the oven to 200 degrees F.

Whisk the cocoa with the powdered sugar in a small bowl. In a large bowl, start beating the egg whites at medium speed. When they are foamy, add the cream of tartar and continue beating, gradually sprinkling in the sugar. Then beat at high speed for 5–10 minutes, until the meringue is very stiff and shiny. Now drop in the red food coloring, sift the cocoa-flavored powdered sugar over the top, and delicately fold the mixture together with a rubber scraper.

To make your rock formations, you can use either a pastry bag with a half-inch plain or star decorating tip, or a zip-type plastic freezer bag with one corner snipped off and fitted with a decorating tip (or used plain). You can also form boulders and buttes with a spoon. (For artistic inspiration, I find it helpful to look at pictures of the Grand Canyon and Four Corners area.) Make a variety of shapes, some long and flat and some rounded and thick. This is an ample amount of meringue, so you may also wish to form some of it into disks or "nests" for serving fruit or ice cream.

Bake the meringues for 2 hours without opening the oven door. Then test for doneness; meringue should be dry throughout (but not brown) and easy to nudge off the paper. Probably this will take another 30–60 minutes. Then turn off the oven and let the meringues cool inside it before removing them to a rack. Alternatively, bake the meringues for 1 hour, turn off the oven, and let them dry there overnight. Meringues are very sensitive to humidity, so they should be wrapped airtight and stored in a dry place, where they will keep for up to 6 months. (For short-term storage, a cool oven may be your best choice.)

Colorado River Sauce or "Chocolate Soup"

These two chocolate sauces have different textures, and our family can't agree which is best. The first variation is more candy-like and will string up and then crystallize on ice cream, especially when the sauce has been reheated. The second has a waxier, lusher, creamier texture.

Chocolate Fudge Sauce

MAKES 2½ CUPS

½ cup cocoa

1½ cups sugar

⅔ cup white corn syrup

⅔ cup water

2 ounces unsweetened chocolate, chopped

6 tablespoons butter

½ cup cream

2 teaspoons vanilla extract

⅛ teaspoon salt

Whisk together the cocoa and sugar in a small bowl. In a small heavy saucepan, boil the corn syrup until it thickens slightly and becomes stringy, about 2 minutes. Off heat, add the water, and then the cocoa and sugar mixture, and return the pot to the heat. Simmer the sauce, stirring, until the sugar crystals all dissolve. Then add the chocolate and stir until it melts. Next add the butter and the cream, stir well, and bring to a full boil for 15 seconds, watching and stirring very carefully. Off heat, add the vanilla and the salt.

Serve either hot or lukewarm. Sealed in a jar, this sauce keeps indefinitely under refrigeration. To reheat, either use a microwave (high power for 15–20 seconds; stir midway) or place the jar in a pan of water and simmer, stirring occasionally, until the sauce liquifies.

Chocolate Cream Sauce

MAKES 3½ CUPS

2 cups cream

½ cup dark brown sugar

3 tablespoons unsalted butter

2 ounces unsweetened chocolate, chopped

8 ounces bittersweet chocolate, chopped

Pinch of salt

2 teaspoons vanilla extract, or 2 tablespoons dark rum

In a 2-quart saucepan, bring the cream to a boil, watching very carefully so it does not boil over. Now simmer it for 15–20 minutes, until it is reduced to about 1 cup. Add the brown sugar and stir until it is completely dissolved. Then, off heat, stir in the butter, the two kinds of chocolate, the salt, and the vanilla or rum.

Serve, store, and reheat in the same way as Chocolate Fudge Sauce.

ASSEMBLE THE GRAND CANYON CAKE Line the bottom and sides of a 9-inch springform pan with wax paper cut to fit (round for the bottom, a strip or strips for the sides). Using a long serrated knife, slice the cake horizontally in thirds. French and Italian pastry chefs would sprinkle the layers at this point with liqueur-flavored syrup, but children—and adults—often dislike this flavor and texture, so I usually omit it or substitute a thin layer of chocolate or fruit sauce, which adds to the stratified look. Freeze the sliced cake for an hour or so to firm it up, and soften the ice cream in the refrigerator for about 20 minutes.

Place a layer of cake in the bottom of the pan. Spread on a layer of ice cream, followed by another layer of cake and so forth, ending with a layer of ice cream. To layer more than one flavor of ice cream, you may need to freeze the first one briefly before adding the second. Wrap the cake well, and freeze it for at least 6 hours.

DECORATE AND SERVE Remove the cake from the pan, and transfer it to a platter. Covered, it can wait in the freezer until just before serving. First, soften the cake for 15–20 minutes in the refrigerator. Then, breaking and crumbling them to create a natural effect, arrange the meringue buttes and boulders on the top and around the bottom edge of the cake, along with candy rocks and pebbles. Dust the cake and platter decoratively with cocoa, using a small fine sieve. Garnish each serving of the canyon with a little chocolate river and a few rocks.

Recipe Index